Ayn Rand

Masterworks in the Western Tradition

Nicholas Capaldi and Stuart Warner
General Editors

Vol. 5

PETER LANG
New York • Washington, D.C./Baltimore • Boston • Bern
Frankfurt am Main • Berlin • Brussels • Vienna • Canterbury

Tibor R. Machan

Ayn Rand

PETER LANG
New York • Washington, D.C./Baltimore • Boston • Bern
Frankfurt am Main • Berlin • Brussels • Vienna • Canterbury

3 1257 01406 2524

Library of Congress Cataloging-in-Publication Data

Machan, Tibor R.
Ayn Rand / Tibor R. Machan.
p. cm. — (Masterworks in the Western tradition; vol. 5)
Includes bibliographical references and index.
1. Rand, Ayn—Criticism and interpretation. 2. Women and literature—United States—
History—20th century. 3. Philosophy in literature. 4. Objectivism
(Philosophy). 5. Rand, Ayn—Philosophy. I. Title. II. Series.
PS3535.A547Z78   813'.52—dc21   99-28015
ISBN 0-8204-4144-9
ISSN 1086-539X

Die Deutsche Bibliothek-CIP-Einheitsaufnahme

Machan, Tibor R.:
Ayn Rand / Tibor R. Machan.
–New York; Washington, D.C./Baltimore; Boston; Bern;
Frankfurt am Main; Berlin; Brussels, Vienna; Canterbury: Lang.
(Masterworks in the Western tradition; Vol. 5)
ISBN 0-8204-4144-9

Cover design by Nona Reuter

The paper in this book meets the guidelines for permanence and durability
of the Committee on Production Guidelines for Book Longevity
of the Council of Library Resources.

© 1999, 2001 Peter Lang Publishing, Inc., New York

Printed in the United States of America

For Kate

Acknowledgments

Some of the work in this book is drawn from essays that have appeared in *The Occasional Review, Objectivity, The International Review of Social Economics*, and *Full Context*, and in Douglas Rasmussen and Douglas J. Den Uyl's *The Philosophic Thought of Ayn Rand*. I thank the editors for permission to use this material.

Many people have helped me with this project, among them Douglas B. Rasmussen, Douglas J. Den Uyl, Eric Mack, Mark Turiano, Barbara Branden, Fred D. Miller, Jr., Daniel Shapiro, et al. Roger E. Bissell, J. Roger Lee, and Chris Sciabarra read and offered detailed comments on an earlier version of the manuscript. In all cases I am responsible for how they helped to shape the final text.

I wish also to thank the Hoover Institution on War, Revolution and Peace, at Stanford University, for providing me with a research fellowship to work on this book and on other projects. I am especially grateful to executive director John Raisian for his support of my scholarly efforts. And I thank Mandy MacCalla for her support and friendship. I also wish to thank my sister, Kati MacHan, for her editorial assistance. Bernadette Alfaro at Peter Lang offered much help with my deskpublishing efforts.

Table of Contents

Preface

Ayn Rand, born Alissa Zinovievna Rosenbaum on February 2, 1905, in St. Petersburg, Russia, emigrated to the United States after her education at the University of Petrograd, in 1926. After a brief stay with relatives in Chicago, she moved to Hollywood to immerse herself in the film industry as a screenwriter. Rand became a citizen in 1931. She was a wardrobe girl at a major studio when she started to work in films.

Rand died on March 6, 1982, in New York City. She was buried in Valhalla, New York, next to the grave of her husband, who died four years earlier.

Like many others—Marx, Nietzsche, Freud, Wittgenstein, Popper, and Sartre—Rand became surrounded by admirers and *epigone*. Nietzsche once said that we must forgive all great thinkers their first disciples. This may be less true of Rand, who actively encouraged the loyalty such persons were too willing to offer, yet who later broke free of her psychological and intellectual supervision. As noted, Rand isn't unique in this—many innovative thinkers find that they become guardians of a flock of people who imagine in them a savior, someone who showed them a way, right or wrong.

This project is neither hostile nor fawning. Nor is this a comprehensive critical assessment of Ayn Rand's philosophy; more an introduction of her ideas to a broader readership who may have heard of Rand but not examined her ideas in detail.

The book begins with an introduction that gives a bare outline of Rand's ideas and a description of her major fiction. It is followed by a longer discussion and outline of Rand's philosophy of Objectivism. Next I present the most vital portion of Rand's philosophy, her understanding of axiomatic concepts and propositions. This is the foundation of her epistemology, resting on what she regards as axioms, indispensable ideas; it's also the area of philosophy in which she carried out the most focused and detailed work. Rand's legacy, her Objectivist epistemology, is the core of the book.

I will also examine Rand's moral philosophy of ethical egoism, an ethics unique in its combination of ancient and modern moral philosophy. The following chapter deals in greater detail with Randian social philosophy, her rational individualism. Then I compare Rand to Marx; given her emphatic rejection of both dialectical materialism and collectivist politics, this will provide a good contrast between Rand's ideas and others that have been prominent in contemporary intellectual circles. A brief explanation of Rand's philosophical and moral contempt for Immanuel Kant follows. I conclude the book with a discussion of missing or unfinished areas and problems in Rand's philosophical thinking.

I believe this will do justice to our subject, an introduction to Ayn Rand's philosophical thought.[1]

Endnotes

[1] I became aware of Ayn Rand when I was a young man in the U. S. Air Force. I read her novels *The Fountainhead* and *Atlas Shrugged*. The former inspired me, the latter provoked me to a good deal of reflection. Several of us stayed up into many weekend nights at Andrews Air Force Base, in the summer of 1962, examining the philosophical themes covered in Galt's famous speech.

Although I kept reading Rand's work afterward, even attended a few lectures given by her one-time student and disciple, Nathaniel Branden, I kept away from what came to be called "the inner circle." Eventually, after an exchange of correspondence, I was declared *persona non grata* by Branden and thereafter had no fruitful contact with her or those surrounding her. I proceeded, however, throughout my career in academic philosophy, to study her works and to begin to develop some of her ideas as I understood them.

One advantage to having been "blackballed" is that I owed no personal loyalty to Rand or anyone near her. Yet, neither did I discard her ideas, just because we couldn't cooperate and because I was cast out of the fold. There are certain advantages, both intellectual and psychological, to being set adrift: One can be comfortable both admiring and critically assessing the achievements of the person who helped one look at the world with philosophical profit.

Introduction:
Ayn Rand, Iconoclast

Iconoclast to the Core

Ayn (Ai-en) Rand called herself a novelist-philosopher. She became immensely popular as the former and recently has been gaining respect as the latter.

Rand came to the United States from Russia in 1926, at age 21. Her work consists mainly of novels and nonfiction essays, although she has also written published and unpublished plays and short stories. The novels that gained her prominence are *The Fountainhead* (1943) and *Atlas Shrugged* (1957). Her earlier novels, *We the Living* (1936) and *Anthem* (1938), were published initially in England but not celebrated until the appearance of the later ones. Rand's stage play *The Night of January 16th* (1933-68) achieved success on Broadway and the amateur theater circuit. *The Fountainhead* was made into a movie starring Gary Cooper and Patricia Neal.

Rand also left her mark on several movie scripts, most notably *Love Letters*, a film starring Joseph Cotten. Her nonfiction works are collections of essays taken mainly from her journals, *The Objectivist Newsletter* and *The Objectivist*, some original essays and various excerpts from her novels. Ayn Rand's major nonfiction works are *For the New Intellectual* (1961), *The Virtue of Selfishness* (1964), *Capitalism, the Unknown Ideal* (1966), *The Romantic Manifesto* (1969), *The New Left: The Anti-Industrial Revolution* (1971), *Introduction to Objectivist Epistemology* (1979) ,and the posthumously published *Philosophy: Who Needs It* (1982). *For the New Intellectual* includes a long historical narrative, in which Rand outlines the central archetypes that move human history, and excerpts from each of her novels. The other works include mostly philosophical and cultural commentaries by Rand and others who have contributed to her journals. Her most important philosophical book, *Introduction to Objectivist Epistemology*, was expanded by Leonard Peikoff and republished in 1985. The later edition includes an essay by Peikoff and a lengthy transcript of conversations she had with various philosophers regarding her epistemological views.

Several pamphlets have been published which are either reprints of essays from the journals or transcripts of lectures Rand or her associates have delivered at colleges and universities across the USA. Since her death in 1982 several other collections of both her fictional and nonfiction works have appeared, as well as studies of her writings by critics, sympathizers, devotees and non-partisan scholars.

This book will focus on Ayn Rand's philosophical ideas, so we will not deal at length with her literary accomplishments. However, here are a few paragraphs describing her major fiction, the four novels that are still selling well and being translated into more and more languages.

We the Living

This work is the closest Rand came to an autobiographical novel. It tells the story of Kira, a beautiful young woman eager to save the life of her sick and dejected beloved in the new Soviet Union. She becomes entangled with a communist whose ideas she detests but whom she respects for his earnestness. The work is episodic, not at all like Rand's later blockbuster novels. It reads more like novels of the period, without her philosophical ideas presented explicitly. Only now and then does the reader glimpse what is to come from Rand, as when she lays out the objections to communism's anti-individualist stance.[1]

Anthem

This novella is one of the most poignant dystopias, dealing with a society in which individuality is a crime and everyone must speak in the first person plural. Then one unbroken individual rediscovers books using the word "I." The high point of the story is when this person makes his declaration of independence, his anthem. Unlike Aldous Huxley's *Brave New World* or George Orwell's *1984*, technology, science and everything else that depends on human creativity stagnates. Rand realized by then that she wanted to make the point that without individuality and the right to individual liberty, all the spheres of human thought and action are adversely affected, if not destroyed. That coercion, e.g., government regimentation, impedes or paralyzes the mind was already implicit in this work.[2]

The Fountainhead

The Fountainhead made Rand a best-selling author. It contains a relatively mature version of her philosophical thought, at least in the spheres of morality and politics. A young architect struggles to uphold his integrity as a principled professional in the face of an intelligentsia that despises individual excellence and independence of thought. Howard Roark is the hero and his nemesis is Elsworth Toohey, a popular columnist and evil genius who wants to destroy Roark. All the characters are distinct moral types. Dominique Francon is the love interest and tragic figure who does not want Roark to win because she has basically given up on the human race. Peter Keating is the second-hander, to use Rand's term for a spineless person who gains esteem only through pleasing others. Gail Wynand is a conflicted, pragmatic publisher, who is ambitious, productive, and otherwise much admired by Roark but who will not resist the temptation to pander to the worst tastes of the masses for the greater good.

In *The Fountainhead*, Roark gives a powerful statement of Rand's ethical position, rational egoism. A philosophically relevant aspect of *The Fountainhead* is that by the time Rand writes her magnum opus, *Atlas Shrugged*, she no longer seems to believe that a man such as Elsworth Toohey could exist—anyone as broadly focused, self aware and brilliant could not be so thoroughly evil (although, of course, brilliant evil people, whose focus is sharp but narrow, such as Stadler Ferris in *Atlas Shrugged*, are possible).[3]

Atlas Shrugged

Ayn Rand's major literary achievement, *Atlas Shrugged*, is a book of more than one thousand pages, published by Random House, at the time the most prestigious publisher in America. No brief summary can do justice to its scope. On one level, it is a mystery that tries to solve the puzzle of what makes the world work when it does work, who are the individuals who manage to make it work, and why.

Ultimately Rand's answer is her philosophy of Objectivism, with the emphasis on its ethics and politics, although other branches are discussed as well in the famous speech delivered by John Galt, the novel's protagonist, at the brink of the collapse of the United States.

The plot of *Atlas Shrugged* is that the US—indeed, the globe—is becoming a collectivist hell, mostly what we know as a robust welfare state in which collective rights—to health care, welfare, and so on, and so forth—are the basis of government. Need justifies subduing those with talent and ambition. One man, Galt, realizes that the only chance to set things right is to withdraw the mental labors of those who are the world's motor—rational, thoughtful, focused, and productive individuals. The drama concerns bringing around the very best people in the country to see the problem and do the right thing about it. The theme is that the human mind is the motor of our world.

Atlas Shrugged's cast of characters is considerable; each represents a certain moral-psychological type. (In Rand's philosophy, psychology is very much a normative field, except perhaps when it addresses extremely damaged, incapacitated individuals.) Many of them present at least an outline of their ideas, admirable or vile, with the main monologue, in the form of a radio talk, given by Galt himself. In this talk we find the outlines of Objectivism. It runs sixty pages in the hard-cover version. When Rand was urged to cut it by her editor-publisher, Random House's Bennett Cerf, her response was "Would you cut parts of the Bible?"

Whether Rand was the great novelist she and her admirers believed her to be is not something to be considered here. Suffice to note that millions have read and continue to read her works and a significant percent find Rand's ideas sufficiently convincing to begin to study and develop her philosophy of Objectivism further.

Rand's fiction is written in a traditional style, one not widely embraced by the literati of our time. Victor Hugo and Feodor Dostoyevsky were her literary models. It is no wonder then that contemporary critics who tend to champion the likes of Joyce, Celine, Capote and Updike would not find her up to snuff. Yet Rand's philosophical and political impact has made it difficult for them to ignore her. She has come in for considerable criticism as a novelist. Often, however, it is unclear whether what critics find objectionable about her is her writing or her iconoclastic views.[4]

One contemporary philosopher, J. Roger Lee, who has worked extensively within the analytical tradition of contemporary academic philosophy, expressed view of Rand *qua* philosopher. It is the view borne out by the following the rest of this work.

I've been impressed by the way that the technical language of the late '60s, language that is largely idiosyncratic to her, factors into her 1950s writing of *Atlas Shrugged*. You've heard me lecture (to a dismissive commentator) that the key term, "fundamental," from the concept formation material in *Introduction to Objectivist Epistemology*, is used by her in a technically correct way in her eleven-years-earlier metaethical work, to whit, 'there is only one fundamental alternative....' And remember that the metaethics argument is a transcendental (stolen concept) argument of the sort that is supposed to show that the concept of value is impossible unless ... fundamental .... Furthermore, in *Atlas Shrugged*, when Dagny Taggart is noting her impression of John Galt, she uses just the language that Ayn Rand uses over ten years later in the chapter on axiomatic concepts in *IOE* (the language is one Aristotle might have used) about the perceptible form, but it has Ayn Rand's unique spin on it, namely, that analysis of [identification of] what she already knows will disclose the rest: 'She noticed that she had asked questions about every subject, but not about him. It was as if he were a single whole, grasped by her first glance at him, like some irreducible absolute, like an axiom not to be explained any further, as if she knew everything about him by direct perception, and what awaited her now was only the process of identifying her knowledge.' (704)

The net effects of both of these points is that: (1) she was always a lot more technically integrated than she is given credit for, and (2) there was a lot going on, of commitments in abstract technical philosophy that is not to be found in the published journals.[5]

Endnotes:

[1] Yet as a novel this is a considerable achievement. As the late Ron Merrill put it, "Purely in terms of literary technique, *We the Living* is an absolutely extraordinary first novel. That a beginning writer, working in a language not her own, could produce a book so complex, subtle, skillfully structured, and emotionally powerful, and in the process deal with important philosophical and political themes in an original manner, marks her at once as a genius." *The Ideas of Ayn Rand* (LaSalle, IL: Open Court Publishing Co., Inc., 1991), p. 33.

[2] Daryll Wright, "Reason and Freedom in Ayn Rand's Politics," paper presented at The Ayn Rand Society Annual Meeting, American Philosophical Association, Eastern Division, Philadelphia, PA, December 28, 1997. See, also, Professor Douglas J. Den Uyl's insightful response to this paper which further clarifies Rand's critique of coercion as an impediment to full consciousness.

[3] For an excellent discussion of this novel, see Douglas J. Den Uyl, *The Fountainhead, An American Novel* (Boston, MA: Twayne, 1999).

[4] For those who would like to discover Ayn Rand's philosophical pedigree as well as a good deal about her life, two books will be of considerable help. First,

Barbara Branden, *The Passion of Ayn Rand* (Doubleday, 1986) is a good introduction. Next, Christopher Sciabarra, *Ayn Rand, The Russian Radical* (Penn State University Press, 1995) deals with the historical and philosophical origins and meaning of many of Rand's ideas. In consequences of the latter work, Ayn Rand's ideas could begin to acquire a serious scholarly reputation, by virtue of the detailed study of its origins and content presented in Sciabarra's book. It brings to light information about Rand's philosophical education that is not available elsewhere and shows that this education was substantial. The author shows that Rand spoke to ancient and modern philosophical concerns and did so in a unique fashion, something reminiscent of only one school of modern philosophical thought, namely, existentialism. (Sartre, Camus, and some others also produced both systematic philosophy as well as dramatization of their philosophical ideas in plays and novels, akin to what Rand accomplished.) Only in the case of Rand this intellectual immersion in both literature and formal philosophy came in support of a unique synthesis of philosophical ideas that have not previously received such treatment. As will be seen in this work, Rand attempts to develop the idea and drama of an essentially reasonable, nonabsurdist, nonmystical outlook on reality.

For an up-to-date report on scholarly work focusing on Ayn Rand's contributions to philosophy and literature, see Christopher Sciabarra, "A Renaissance in Rand Scholarship," *Reason Papers*, #23. For a very insightful discussion of the evolution and maturation of Ayn Rand's thinking, see Stephen Cox's review of *Journals of Ayn Rand* in *Liberty*, June 1998.

5   J. Roger Lee, electronic mail post, August 10, 1998.

Chapter 1:
Intellectual Iconoclast

Following Her Own Beat

Just reflecting on the titles of her books gives a clue to the iconoclasm of Ayn Rand. Objectivism—what most would call a type of realism[1]—in metaphysics, a contextualism in epistemology, egoism in morality, capitalism in politics, romantic-realism in literature: these are ways of understanding the world that are largely foreign to our era.

In contrast, the dominant metaphysics in our time has been, well, no metaphysics at all. After some crucial implications of René Descartes' thought and the explicit views of Immanuel Kant, a great many leading philosophers have accepted that metaphysics is impossible or irrelevant—in any case, secondary. Since, or so many prominent philosophers think, we are unable to examine the world independently of how our own thinking influences it, we are not really able to have confidence in what we take to be its essential structure or principles. Thus for many, metaphysical claims turn out to be cultural or even personal prejudices, an ideology in the Marxian sense of that term.

In epistemology, the orthodoxy now tends to be social subjectivism or what Richard Rorty calls solidarity—criteria of truth established by one's group, culture, tribe, or community. This because rationally based objectivity isn't supposed to be possible to us whose minds condition our awareness. We can't "climb out of our minds" to make sure our mind's contents correctly match reality; there is no "skyhook—something which might lift us out of our beliefs,"[2] as we figure out the cognitive relationship we have to the rest of the world. In contrast, Rand's epistemology is based on the efficacy of human reason in the task of grasping objective reality.

In ethics, there is little doubt that philosophers who take it seriously champion altruism or utilitarianism. For example, as W. G. Maclagan tells us, in his essay defending the position, that "'Altruism' [is] assuming a duty to relieve the distress and promote the happiness of our fellows.... Altruism is to...maintain quite simply that a man may and should discount altogether his own pleasure or happiness as such when he is deciding what course of action to pursue."[3] That such unselfishness is deemed morally superior to other approaches to living is evident throughout much of the world's ethical opinion and in all forms of literature (wherein moral dramas are played out to various degrees of sophistication).[4]

The main trends in political philosophy among the central players in the discipline are, even after the fall of the USSR, some version of socialism—democratic or "market" types—or communitarianism. Some inroad has been made by classical liberal ideas, especially since the publication of Robert Nozick's *Anarchy, State, and Utopia* (Basic Books) twenty-five years ago. And at public-policy levels, free market ideas have become widely championed. But in academe the collectivist trend continues.

There is no widely accepted idea in the field of aesthetics but certainly no appreciation of romanticism in serious literature is evident anywhere except in some fringe circles.

Accordingly, Rand's challenge to trends in her time reaches to the most fundamental issues in philosophy. The same, however, cannot be said about the relationship with ordinary thinking and conduct. Most individuals are realists, when they give the matter some thought. They do not believe in spirits or ghosts or that someone's mind creates the world except, perhaps, in moments of religious reflection. Most go through their days trusting their ability to know the world by means of their normal faculties, although when discussing it they may say something different because in the abstract areas of reflecting about the world, they tend to pick up what the learned say, what they absorb in the high schools and colleges they attend. Even in morality, most individuals act as if a certain type of egoism is guiding their conduct, thinking of their goals and purposes as most important, their families' and friends' following and then those of their neighbors, and so on. They are what Aristotle called lovers of self: "He therefore who loves and indulges the dominant part of himself is a lover of self in the fullest degree."[5] But when they speak out it is unselfishness that most of them praise.

So while Rand is an intellectual iconoclast, she is not some bizarre thinker, such as Bishop George Berkeley, Jean-Paul Sartre, or Paul Feyerabend—to name a few spanning the past few centuries—whose ideas are anything but in accord with what most individuals take to be obviously true. This may account for why Ayn Rand is a popular novelist but not popular among philosophers, and not even given due respect for her clarity of thought, let alone the content of her thinking.

A Novelist-Philosopher

Ayn Rand called herself a novelist/philosopher. In her essay "The Goal of My Writing," she explained that she wanted to be a novelist from the age of nine. She later found that the worldview which she sought to express was missing from, even denigrated within, her intellectual climate. In order to provide for herself the foundation and context within which she could write her romantic realist fiction, she embarked on the task of developing a rational philosophy.

To convey Ayn Rand's unique philosophical work, let me begin with an outline of her philosophy, Objectivism.

Rand divides philosophy into five major branches: metaphysics, epistemology, ethics, politics, and aesthetics. This division is not original with her, but it was, in Rand's time, quite out of favor with most academic philosophers. It is the substance of her philosophy within these several branches that gives a better idea as to why Ayn Rand stands apart from the mainstream of the philosophy of her time.

In metaphysics, Rand's philosophy is not exactly Aristotelian realism; she does not see essences (or abstract definitions) as concretely real—but the world undeniably exists, just as in Aristotle's view, independent of what anyone may feel or think about it. It is what it is, period. Existence or reality is acknowledged at the outset, so that the concept of "existence" is axiomatic, undeniable, and necessary—"existence exists," as expressed in propositional form. That fact is evident in any meaningful thought, action, or communication. (We shall later take a closer look at Rand's axiomatic concepts, which comprise a major element of her philosophy.)

No Prior Certainty of Consciousness

Unlike many prominent (academic) philosophers in her day, Rand does not consider epistemology the first field of philosophical inquiry. To do so would be to accept what Rand calls "the prior certainty of consciousness." That is to say, considering consciousness as the first thing we are aware of in reality is a mistake. So epistemology – with its central question, "What is the nature of knowledge?" – is not the primary field of philosophy.

To focus attention on the faculty of awareness prior to acknowledging the existence of that which is the object of awareness is impossible, according to Rand. Awareness cannot be prior to what one can be aware of – *pace* René Descartes – since awareness presupposes something that a consciousness can be aware of. To put it more simply, we know, in part, because there are things to be known, so knowledge cannot be the first item on the list of what there is. Thus, the field that investigates the fundamental nature of what exists – that is, what there is to be aware of – must be prior in content, significance, and logic to the field that asks how it is possible to be aware of something.

This can be appreciated on a commonsense level, too. Much of reality had been around prior to the emergence of those beings capable of awareness.[6] That alone indicates why metaphysics, the study of the nature of the basic facts of reality, precedes epistemology, the study of awareness or consciousness of reality.

Those who contend otherwise will argue, however, that for those beings who are aware, namely, ourselves, the fact of our being aware is prior to anything we are aware of. To put it slightly differently, we know ourselves as knowing even apart from what it is that we know – we are self-aware before aware of anything else, just because we are generating understanding and this act is itself primary for us. Or, to put it in a way used by some philosophers, our subjectivity is the primary datum for us, with the actual world lying "out there" and thus having a secondary status in the order of awareness. Yet these views are patently self-contradictory by virtue of affirming real things about us that surely were prior to anyone having figured them out.

There are others, certain members of the Idealist school – including some with a serious theological orientation – who hold that the fact that reality can be understood by a mind such as ours shows that it is fundamentally constituted by a structure of ideas or concepts. Consider that as we understand the world, ourselves included, we do this by means of ideas. (Just consider how confusing it is to enter some Middle Eastern bazaars full of objects we don't recognize.) From considerations such as these, Idealists conclude that a mind must be prior to actual things. If not our own minds, at least the mind of God — or Mind Itself or Soul or Reason — is prior to concrete facts.

This position is implicit in nearly all religious viewpoints, and Hegel, who adhered to a version of it, actually thought of Christianity as a simplified, publicly accessible version of Idealism.

Yet, all of this is a mistake, according to Rand. In knowing ourselves as knowing, as being aware, there must already be an acknowledgment of the reality of something that can be known — even if this something is some aspect of ourselves — otherwise we couldn't be aware of (that is, what we would be doing is not knowing something) and thus be aware of ourselves as knowing. Putting it plainly, again, knowledge implies something knowable apart from knowing itself. An example might be pointing — to understand pointing we must first understand that there are those things at which we can point. Without targets at which we can point, pointing would be incomprehensible.

And this goes for knowing. To know requires something to be known. Minds are not containers of objects — minds can know objects, in part, because they have evolved to depend on this knowledge. Anything that couldn't grasp existent beings with the mind would ultimately perish from lack of skills, which are all based on some measure of understanding. (It is something along these lines that Ludwig Feuerbach argued against Hegel, thus earning the respect of naturalist philosophers of all kinds, including Marx — whose naturalism even Rand seemed to respect in contrast, say, to that of Alexander Solzhenitsyn's idealism.) Let Rand make this point herself:

> If nothing exists, there can be no consciousness: a consciousness with nothing to be conscious of is a contradiction in terms. A consciousness conscious of nothing but itself is a contradiction in terms: before it could identify itself as consciousness, it had to be conscious of something....[7]

Metaphysics as First Philosophy

So Rand claims that metaphysics is the first philosophical branch of knowledge or discipline. And in Rand's exploration of epistemology she attests to this fact by recognizing the axiomatic status of the concept "existence" and the resulting proposition "existence exists," ones that basically refer to reality.

Let me summarize what I will be exploring at some length later: Rand states, "Existence exists—and the act of grasping that statement implies two corollary axioms: that something exists which one perceives and that one exists possessing consciousness, consciousness being the faculty of perceiving that which exists."[8] In other words, that existence exists implies that things of a certain kind exist (that something exists which is a certain kind of something), and that one is capable of perceiving that things of various kinds exist (that one is conscious or possesses the faculty of awareness), but with all these as part of the natural world.

The Aristotelian characteristics of this position are reflected in the fact that the basic axiom is a first principle of existence. It expresses in a different form the basic laws of being in Aristotelian metaphysics. The laws of non-contradiction, identity, and excluded-middle are in Aristotle's philosophy axioms—first principles of reality, of being as such. Axioms for Rand take a similar position of priority, the first two as facts of nature and all three as items of knowledge. (The axioms are prior to all the rest of human knowledge, but not in self-conscious knowledge—so that while, logically speaking, everyone must accept the axioms, in fact people may not know and may even deny that they accept them, despite the inconsistency of such a denial.)

Rand also rejects any kind of mind-body dualism and sees the human mind as an aspect of the entire individual human being, not some separate entity occupying a superior status in every human being. It is this aspect of her metaphysics that has very serious and iconoclastic implications for ethics and politics—for example, her construal of productivity as one of the highest virtues and her view that the right to private property is a full fledged feature of the right to liberty.

Several consequences are implied by the Randian metaphysical stance. For Rand the nature of reality—what is central, crucial, essential about existence—does not predetermine the kind(s) of things that might exist. As far as this metaphysical position is concerned, there could be many different sorts of things in reality, provided that nothing that exists contradicts anything else—that the existence of any kind of thing is not in contradiction with the existence of any other. Reality does not admit to contradictions, but it does not limit the variety of things that might exist beyond this basic constraint. Furthermore, things can exist without needing to exist necessarily.

Nor is our inability to prove their necessary existence any liability, unless we are dealing with things—for which necessary existence or necessity is a requirement (the laws of being, for example).

One of the results of this way of conceiving of existence is that numerous irrationalist worldviews are rendered impossible. As an example, by reflecting on the metaphysical ideas of such thinkers as Hegel—who was basically an idealist for whom Mind or Reason exists prior to anything else that it could be aware of—and Marx—for whom nothing but (dialectically driven) material reality exists—it is possible to learn that their metaphysical positions could not be sound. It does not mean that nothing such thinkers say could be true, only that the basic elements of their systems of ideas could not be sound. Put more simply: The world isn't the way they say it is.

Another result of this metaphysical position is that reductionism (the idea that everything in nature must be one kind of thing—any apparent deviations are but illusion or apparent variations) is not metaphysically reasonable. (Some call this monism, but that is best used to simply affirm the nature of reality as an integrated whole, one, however, not necessarily composed of the same kind of stuff!)

There are both materialist and idealist reductionists within philosophy. Some argue that everything that exists must be a certain kind of material reality (matter-in-motion, process, atomic material substance). Others argue that everything that exists must be a certain kind of mental reality (consciousness, God's mind, transcendental reason, or will). Neither of these positions squares with Rand's Objectivism, although it could not be ruled out that everything at one time might have consisted of such constituents alone—for example, that at the point of the Big Bang just one kind of substance existed. But this is not what reductionists argue. Their point is that reality consists of just one kind of stuff, although appearances may deceive us to think otherwise.

Finally, a powerful implication of Rand's metaphysics is that it is possible that different kinds of causes exist in nature. In contrast to prominent views of causality—in terms of which only the sort of cause can exist that is involved in an event producing a subsequent event—the Randian metaphysics implies something very different. Since there could be different kinds and types of things in nature, and since the causal relationships into which entities can enter depend upon the nature of the entities involved—i.e., what these beings are—different kinds of causes also could exist. (This notion becomes vital in Rand's defense of free will, as manifest in the individual human being's capacity of causing or initiating his or her own thinking process.)

When one reflects on the metaphysical underpinnings of most of today's social sciences, it is easy to discover how prominent the one-kind-of-causality view is. And a crucial result of it has been that human beings as individuals could not be regarded as capable of initiating (causing) action. They cannot have free will, despite the fact that nothing has been discovered in any field of science that rules it out and there are very good reasons to believe that we possess it.[9]

Thus the bulk of social science literature is deterministic; the findings take it as given that whatever occurs in human affairs must be caused by something other than the individual in question. For individuals are by definition not mere events/processes but also entities of a certain (rational) kind.[10] If only events can be causes—as in event A causes event B—then it would appear that individuals cannot be causes. So human individuals, too, must be construed as basically impotent. Thus all views to the effect that human beings can initiate action (have freedom of the will, can choose) are today widely—though not universally—considered either prescientific and nonsensical or indicative of a dualistic reality containing one realm where causality is operative, another where it is inoperative. Both of these alternatives are rejected via Randian metaphysics.[11]

Objectivism in Epistemology

In epistemology, Rand's views are no less at odds with the bulk of positions advanced by philosophers of her day. In the dominant view then, as they emerge in classes and the professional journals and books, epistemology was construed to be the primary field of philosophy. Therefore, "How do we know reality?" or "What is the nature of knowledge?" are high on the list of questions to be attended to within a comprehensive philosophical inquiry.

It is clear, however, that it is impossible to answer this question if it is the first one, since to answer it one must have a standard by which to determine a correct answer. Without some idea of what counts as correct, the inquiry cannot go far. Indeed, the big problem in epistemology while Rand was doing work in the field is that most theories of knowledge ended in a vicious circle.[12] Unless the metaphysical axioms of what are the basic requirements for something to exist are first identified, the answers to the questions of epistemology cannot be evaluated.

Ayn Rand's *Introduction to Objective Epistemology* dwells on one of the "cardinal elements" of Objectivist epistemology, the Objectivist theory of concepts. The work addresses a standard problem in the history of philosophy, that of universals. The issue, in Rand's terms, is:

> Since man's knowledge is gained and held in conceptual form, the validity of man's knowledge depends on the validity of concepts. But concepts are abstractions or universals, and everything that man perceives is particular, concrete. What is the relationship between abstract and concrete beings? To what precisely do concepts refer in reality? Do they refer to something real, something that exists—or are they merely inventions of man's mind, arbitrary constructs or loose approximations that cannot claim to represent knowledge?[13]

I won't attempt to summarize Rand's solution to this problem here—we will consider it later. For now, understand that her views are in considerable conflict not only with what most philosophers in her era said on the issue, but with the main traditions of modern philosophy on this topic, rationalism and empiricism.

As an example, two prominent ideas of what definitions are have gained currency during the last centuries. One holds that a definition must be a statement of the (timelessly) necessary and sufficient attributes or characteristics of being something of a certain kind, and the other that definitions are statements of conveniently or habitually associated characteristics of things with no firm ground to give them validity. The former viewpoint on definitions renders it impossible that a correct, valid definition could ever require modification or change, thus producing the consequence which is expressed by the latter viewpoint—namely, that correct, valid definitions are impossible. In contrast to these two viewpoints Rand develops her idea of contextual definitions. In Rand's own summary:

> An objective definition, valid for all men, is determined according to all the relevant knowledge available at that stage of mankind's development. Definitions are not changelessly absolute, but they are contextually absolute. A definition is false if it does not specify the known relationships among existents (in terms of the known essential characteristics) or if it contradicts the known.[14]

16

And it will help to add another summary point from her work.

> A definition is the *condensation* of a vast body of observations — and its validity depends on the truth or falsehood of these observations, as represented and summed up by the designation of a concept's essential, defining, characteristic(s).[15]

Even without elaborate study one can pinpoint the crucial differences between Rand's ideas about definitions and the view of most philosophers writing at the time. Rand speaks of definitions being true or false. Most philosophers rejected this and had argued, instead, that definitions may be useful or useless, accepted or unaccepted, stipulated or not, but not firmly, objectively grounded in reality. Since by the tenets of most early twentieth century philosophies a definition states what has been put together as a matter of convenience, decision, or fiat, the question of whether definitions are true or false cannot arise.

Definitions are admitted to serve an important role in any theory, but it is also held that despite their importance there is no objective relationship between such definitions and reality. The reason for this stance is that within many philosophers' views of knowledge it would never be possible for us to tell whether the characteristics of some concept which we have identified as essential really are such characteristics.

In summary, there is widespread skepticism about man's capacity to know the world, including the essential characteristics of the existents that populate the world, not to mention the principles that ought to guide us in our voluntary conduct. Rand's theory of definitions is the result of an entirely different view of human knowledge and stands in opposition to early and mid-twentieth-century philosophy, including its embrace of the alleged dichotomy between knowing that something *is* the case and that one *ought* to do this or that.

Accordingly, for many philosophers, definitions are tautologies, necessary truths "by stipulation" and as such tell us nothing about reality (since any concept we use for thinking or talking about the world is not definable as a tautology or necessary truth). What appear to be exceptions, namely, geometry and law, are supposed to consist of concepts that are part of a system constructed by human beings, which is to say, stipulated.

For most philosophers of her time, then, what is known of the real world is not definable—of concepts that group units on the basis, to use Ludwig Wittgenstein's famous term, only a "family resemblance." In formal (stipulated) systems, we can have definitions that meet the criteria of stating a necessary truth or tautology, but these, in turn, fail to refer to anything real.

Rand rejects this idea. She believes that all concepts can be defined, though not as simply as some philosophers would suggest. She poses the rhetorical question, to make this point, "[W]hy are square circle' or 'male aunt' logically impossible, but 'life without oxygen' is not? Merely because 'square,' 'circle,' 'male' and 'aunt' use simple, almost single-attribute concepts, which do not require a long chain of prior, precise, specific concepts with unequivocal, absolute definitions? Logic, therefore, stops and breaks with reality at the point where a retarded mind (or an anti-effort mind) begins to waver, cloud and vacillate."[16]

For Rand, then, all definitions are contextual but some, because of the simplicity of the concepts being defined, may appear to be more rigorously definable than others. Yet this is because with complex concepts many of us do not sustain the effort to keep up a precise integrating and differentiating process: conceptualization. In fact, she argues, no definitions need to have this attribute of ambiguity. In principle all could be rigorous, precise, albeit contextual. And in many sciences that is just what they are, however far removed they may be from direct perceptual evidence.[17]

Other philosophers have, therefore, misunderstood the nature of definitions, thinking that some of them are stipulated and rigorous, others empirical, thus loose or vague. While they hold to a dualistic view of definitions, Rand holds that definitions are all, in principle, capable of having the same features, stating what—within the range of our awareness of the world—constitutes the essential attributes of what is being defined, moving from the simple to the more and more abstract ones.

Many other features of Rand's epistemology could be discussed, but the above will suffice for illustrating her unorthodox stance. It should be noted, however, that since Ayn Rand's death, philosophy has undergone considerable turmoil. When Ayn Rand first advanced her ideas, a powerful orthodoxy was in the way of positivism and neo-positivism (including pragmatism). Today there is far more experimentation, including a renewed interest in lines of thought that are closer to Rand's than the prevailing orthodoxies were. Aristotelianism is being revived, metaphysics is getting another hearing, and skepticism is struggling with powerful challenges.

Yet, even with these trends, Rand stands out as a uniquely systematic contemporary philosopher. Her work is not, however, as detailed as the works of traditional philosophers; she has simply not spent as much space developing her ideas as did Plato, Aristotle, Spinoza, or Kant. (At least her written work is restricted to dealing with some essentials.) To see how her systematic approach to philosophy is manifested, we can now turn to Rand's ethical position.

Ethical Egoism, the Virtue of Selfishness

Objectivism advocates the ethics of rational self-interest. It advocates egoism, although of a type not usually meant when mainstream moral theorists employ the term.[18]

Because many people are familiar with the word "egoism" and few understand its precise meaning, one should be warned that Ayn Rand's egoism is not psychological egoism, not subjective egoism, not hedonistic egoism, not Hobbesian or atomistic egoism, nor, emphatically, egotism. The term that would express Rand's form of egoism best is rational (or, as I have called my rendition of it, *classical*) egoism.[19]

Psychological egoism holds that people are automatically motivated to desire what is in their own interest. This is not a bona fide ethical or moral theory however, because it thereby denies free will.[20] Subjective egoism holds that one should extend one's unique, singular will into the world as far as possible, that one should act to realize one's idiosyncratic desires. This is not a bona fide ethics because it denies that human beings share their human nature, and any system of ethics contains principles applicable to all individuals as human beings. Hedonistic egoism holds that people should do what pleases or satisfies them. Since pleasures are thereby held to be supreme, this is an impoverished ethical system for it disregards the possibility that human beings have proper goals that may require subordinating pleasures. Atomistic or Hobbesian egoism is fully deterministic, based on the view that the self is a bundle of passions driving the individual to achieve their satisfaction. This is not an ethical view because what people are determined to do by forces they cannot control is incapable of being evaluated as right or wrong; what a person cannot help, he cannot take responsibility for.

Of course, a good deal more could be said about each of these positions but the above should suggest why Rand would consider those positions inadequate. In their place — and in the place of all nonegoistic ethics such as utilitarianism, Stoicism, altruism, Kantianism, and so on — Rand proposes her version of ethical egoism.

Ethical or rational egoism is the view that each person should live to achieve his own happiness. The principles of conduct that further the goal of a person's own happiness are moral principles or virtues, the standards for evaluating human actions and institutions. Happiness is identified by reference to human nature, by what it is to be or to live as a successful human being (always to be implemented in one's particular context). Happiness is the "state of non-contradictory joy," a state in which one has realized his set of consistent goals in life.

The standard version of egoism holds that what we should do is determined by what we should get for ourselves, some kind of fulfillment of desires or attainment of benefits. Rand's version of egoism argues that it is a given that human beings have as their proper goal their own happiness, and ethics identifies the principles which when followed will most likely assure them of reaching that goal. Morality, then, is a system of guidelines to be followed to achieve happiness.

Ethical or rational egoism involves numerous philosophical issues in its development as a theory. It must be possible to identify what human nature is; what "self" means in "self-interest" depends on this. It must be possible to identify the nature of happiness and to learn when some particular individual is happy, as well as what principles of conduct serve to achieve that person's happiness.

Most fundamentally, the ethical system Rand advocates is completely dependent for its philosophical support on Objectivist metaphysics and epistemology — for example, her theory of definition recovers the lost ground of Aristotelian-inspired naturalist meta-ethics whereby human nature is seen as the ultimate standard of value. Without that prior theory, naturalism falters seriously.

Rand's ethics aims, of course, to solve some of the standard problems of moral philosophy. For instance, in terms of this system, morality has a rational, objective foundation — namely, the requirements of man's life *qua* man, as a rational animal. Morality is a necessary element of human life, based on the realization that human beings are free to choose what they will do and that they must choose correctly from among numerous alternative options so as to succeed at life as the sort of entities they are. If one chooses to live a human life, one ought to abide by certain principles of conduct.

Moreover, the Objectivist view of happiness, if right, is the proper goal for each individual at any time. This element provides the thesis its universalism. Yet, because of the indefinite ways individual fulfillment may be achieved, this ethics by no means implies that everyone ought to live the same way. While the general goal is happiness, one person's happiness, or the way to attain it, would not be identical to everyone else's.

Even the principles or virtues—that is, the abstract guidelines to how we ought to act (honestly, courageously, prudently, productively, and, most of all, rationally)—may apply differently for different people, depending on time, place, knowledge, and age. Only the cardinal virtue of rationality is universal; other virtues, like courage, may not be possible for some (e.g., paralyzed) persons. Justice is a virtue that applies in a social context, so a man outside of a society may never have occasion to be just. But everyone must choose to exercise his reasoning capacity, for that is the central condition for living life as a human being.

Objectivist egoistic ethics adds a dimension of realism to moral philosophy which that field has lacked since Kant removed it. Kantian ethics held all moral conduct to be motivated by considerations that may well have nothing to do with actual consequences for life on earth. Any regard for one's own life, even for the lives of others, could have nothing to do with morality. Morality had to be concerned with pure principles of reason. (Thus the well-known slogan that what counts is that someone means well, whatever the consequences; or duty for duty's sake.) There are complicated origins to this way of conceiving of morality, not the least being that knowledge of the world was considered to be very tentative, uncertain, and existence itself was considered to be infinitely changeable, so consequences could not be counted on. But one result of the Kantian approach has been that morality and practical concerns have become dichotomized. Realistic people, people with practical concerns, opted for amoralism, rejecting morality as irrelevant to life. Moralists on the other hand were seen as naive idealists.

In Objectivism all this is rejected and morality is shown to be a practical necessity and possibility for human life. But there is a great deal of honest misunderstanding of this point of view. Thus when Objectivist ethics was explained to many philosophers contemporaneous with Rand, they quickly dismissed it as a case of confusing the practical with the moral "ought." (Social scientists did this even more readily in a knee-jerk fashion.) Sure, they said, it is possible to prove statements of the form: "Johnny should take the train" when one has specified that Johnny wants to go to New York the quickest possible way. But moral "ought" refers to means *and* goals. What should Johnny do and how? Or what should he want to do? These are the morally crucial issues.

Objectivism denies the dichotomy. There is a question about what man's goal is, but this is a question of fact: consider what kind of entity is being discussed, namely a rational animal, a living, biological entity with the capacity and requirement to guide his life by way of conceptual thought. The (proper) aim for such a being is to live as long and as well as possible as the kind of being it is. And morality is a code or system of ethics that specifies the principles that make this possible. The only difference between moral and practical (prudential or pragmatic) judgments is that the former specify principles and goals pertaining to every human being, whereas the latter concern varied and specialized circumstances, narrower contexts, and intermediary principles and goals.

Some wish morality to be something else, to have a higher mission than being used to guide human life to a successful completion. Such persons are not interested in a rational solution to the problems of moral philosophy. Such philosophers have already accepted the noumenal/phenomenal — otherwise sometimes referred to as the analytic/synthetic, conceptual/empirical — dichotomy and have cut the world up into two irreconcilable realms, requiring faith in the former pair and reason — science (as in empirical science) in the latter.

Once again, Ayn Rand's position is iconoclastic. Rand, indeed, stands in opposition to more than an academic philosophical trend. Since many more people than professional philosophers get involved in moral advocacy, even meta-ethical commentary, Rand is opposed by all those who either advocate some form of self-denying ethics or deny the meaningfulness of ethics in the first place — which is just about everyone who has any views on the subject.

A Radical for Capitalism

The most irksome iconoclasm of Ayn Rand has turned out to be her unabashed pro-capitalist, free market, or laissez-faire stance in the area of political theory. Rand derives from her egoistic ethics a political theory in the tradition of Lockean natural rights. The case is summarized by Rand as follows:

> If man is to live on earth, it is right for him to use his mind, it is right to act on his own free judgment, it is right to work for his values and to keep the product of his work. If life on earth is his purpose, he has a right to live as a rational being.[21]

This argument for natural rights—to life, liberty, and the pursuit of happiness (including property)—is related to the Greek natural *right* tradition (that focuses on right conduct). Yet, the Greek concern with natural right is distinct from the Lockean natural rights view; it concerns the ethically correct thing to do, not social-political obligation to abstain from initiating for against others![22]

Rand adds some true and valuable premises to the older idea. She considers political theory a sub-field of ethics—the question "How should a human community be organized?" answerable only in terms "How should I, a human being, live my life?" The right way to live is the grounds on which the right principles of social organization and law must be based. The rights of human beings are the principles of community conduct, the basic principles of community action. Douglas Rasmussen and Douglas Den Uyl have dubbed these social "meta-norms," the framework of community life that makes living a morally significant life possible *among others*. So if those in one's community are governed by reference to such rights, one has the necessary conditions for choosing whether to act rightly or wrongly, which is the prime objective of justice. (Of course, Rand also held that ethics is most important for one when apart from society, where one is unaided in one's struggle to flourish.)

Some—including Eric Mack who is rather supportive of Rand's philosophy—have criticized Rand for allegedly confusing the two senses of "right," as between "It is right to do X" and "A has the right to do X." Rand of course sees (though does not sufficiently stress) the difference between the two senses of "right," but also correctly links them. The right things for individuals are the basis for the right things for societies. But to have a right to do something is not the same as its being right to do it. Having a right to do X means that it is wrong for another to take action against someone doing X *and* such action may be resisted. It is right for others to refrain from interfering with one's liberty, although in the more basic ethical sense it may also be wrong for one to choose to do X.

In the Objectivist political theory, as in the Lockean, there could be many ethical improprieties with no legal consequences whatsoever. Only when someone's actions (actually or very probably will) violate the rights of others should their immoral conduct produce retaliatory (legal) responses because then their wrong deeds are also intrusive, interfering with some other person's sphere of responsibility.

Rand believes that such rights derive from the ethics of rational egoism—or the ethics of human flourishing—since it is that school of ethics that guides one to act properly, but doing so must be a matter of choice. Only then can moral credit be earned for it. This, of course, also means that one person's evil deed is not usually preventable by others. Thus, the Objectivist (libertarian)[23] polity is not a utopia, unlike so many others that philosophers have proposed, offering as they do a blueprint for universal human fulfillment or emancipation by means of the structure of community life. The Randian legal system is the kind of polity that promises to provide the framework within which individuals in overlapping communities have the most realistic chance for attaining their own best kind of life on earth, although whether they will is a matter of their own initiative and, of course, some measure of good fortune.

The implication of this political theory for citizenship is that human beings should advocate and implement a free society with inviolate prohibition against all conduct that infringes on the rights of individuals to life, liberty and property.

In terms of Rand's account, a free society for human beings is not simply a free market economy, as many conservatives and even classical liberals—who often reduce all social life to economics—would have it. Nor is it simply a society in which intellectual and artistic conduct are protected against intrusions from the uninvited, as (until the late twentieth century) the modern liberal would have it. The conservatives' compromise ends in the totalitarianism of the fascist state, while the modern liberals' leads to communism or socialism. In either case, the Randian idea implies, the compromise of liberty in favor of controlling some aspect of the lives of human beings must eventually destroy liberty. Nor is democracy any kind of panacea as a bulwark against such a corruption of politics; majorities without sound guidance from ethics and political principles are clearly subject to tyrannical tendencies.

Rand's position succeeds in giving the idea of libertarian polity a thorough philosophical foundation. It reaches all the way to the metaphysical rejection of the mind/body dichotomy, coming through epistemology with the theory of knowledge in terms of which it is shown how moral knowledge is possible, going on to ethics and the egoistic code to guide human life, and culminating in the politics of a free, libertarian social order.

A Romantic Realist

Rand's philosophy extends, of course, to aesthetics as well. Not only does Rand affirm the possibility of aesthetic truth and objective artistic excellence (and degradation, for that matter), but she also affirms a substantive literary aesthetics, a bold romanticism with a realist rational basis to it, thus leading to the affirmation of two features of systems of aesthetics usually found in conflict with each other. Central in Rand's view of art is its role in the life of a thinking animal such as a human being, one with the capacity and vital need for conceptual consciousness in the governance of life.

Romanticism has been placed in opposition to realism because values had been thought to require a departure from reality. But in view of Rand's resolution of this problem she could unhesitatingly affirm the unity of these two aesthetic elements, thereby solving a crucial problem in aesthetics but also setting herself up as being opposed to most major philosophical schools.

Since aesthetics is a normative discipline, seeking as it does standards of artistic excellence, criteria by which to judge art, there is a need for discussing how those standards might be identified. Since many in our age reject the notion that beings have a nature—as in "the nature of human beings," "the nature of governments," or "the nature of art"—standards tend to depend upon subjective factors such as the class or age or culture wherein works of art are created. Indeed, in the postmodern era of the twentieth century, it is passé to even speak of standards. At most one might consider sensibilities, style, finesse, subtlety or such, all pretty divorced from any kind of philosophical foundations.

For Rand, in contrast, there is a clear place for art in human life; thus its standards of excellence have to be established by reference to human nature and human goodness. This suggests that for Rand beauty is far from merely in the eye of the beholder, although the alternative isn't some kind of dogged universalism that pays no attention to human differences. But it remains for others to develop the aesthetics of Objectivism, for Rand did not do so herself.[24]

Rand's Philosophical Influence

What about Rand's influence? She has been influential and successful with a considerable portion of not only the lay reading public but also with a small but prolific group of scholars.

Ayn Rand's novels and books are constant sellers. Still, the literary community has either ignored or scoffed at her, as may be expected. Because she knew early in her life what she wanted and where this could be done with the greatest degree of freedom, Rand immigrated to the USA. There her heretical ideas did not hurt her as they would have, had she remained in the Soviet Union. She did, however, experience ostracism by the intellectual community, just the segment of Western society she argued was suffering from serious deficiencies in our era (a point that others, too, have made in the latter part of the 20th century). She is written about, now and then (such as the lengthy articles by Claudia Roth Pierpont in *The New Yorker* in 1996, and by Jeffrey Sharlet in *The Chronicles of Higher Education* in 1999), but she is studied by only a small percentage of philosophical allies and a few fervid detractors. The kind of scholarly attention paid to Jean Paul Sartre, Albert Camus, Thomas Mann, or John Dos Passos hasn't been accorded her.

Some attribute the shunning of Rand to her lack of literary subtlety, yet no one could call Raymond Chandler or Dashiell Hammett, nor even Sartre or Camus, all that subtle, and each of them receives ample attention, even reverence, from the scholarly community. James Joyce comes to mind as a favorite of contemporary literary scholarship, partly because of the virtuosity with which he fascinated scholars. On the other hand, there are few subtleties in John Updike and Graham Greene, both of whom are also on most lists of the preferred among twentieth century authors.

Our concern, though, is not with Rand's literary achievements. We are focusing on Rand's philosophical work. It does appear, though, that the main reason for the treatment that Rand receives is that her views—her philosophy of life—are anathema to most prominent scholars who would have to support any serious, lasting work that students at reputable universities, and especially graduate schools, might undertake on Rand's work. Some of this has been changing—with the important book by Chris Sciabarra, *Ayn Rand: The Russian Radical* (Pennsylvania State University, 1995) and the work he edited with Mimi Reisel Gladstein, *Feminist Interpretations of Ayn Rand* (Pennsylvania State University Press, 1998), as well as, earlier, Doug Rasmussen and Douglas Den Uyl's collection of studies of Rand's philosophical works, *The Philosophic Thought of Ayn Rand* (University of Illinois Press, 1984) and Den Uyl's more recent *The Fountainhead, An American Novel* (Twayne, 1999). But it would be premature to claim that Rand is now the focus of serious, measured, intense scholarly attention around the academic world.

Still, in the professional or academic philosophy journals Rand does not fare anywhere as well as, say, Bertrand Russell or, especially, Ludwig Wittgenstein, she has spawned some serious work throughout this community. In addition, there are or have been specialized journals, such as *Objectivity*—edited by Stephen C. Boyton—in which Rand's work is the animating idea for most papers, while others such as *Reason Papers*—edited by myself—pay frequent attention to works that develop or criticize Rand's ideas. Any serious student of Rand needs to take a look at the wide array of topics with which the authors of *Objectivity* grapple, as well as at some of the study groups in cyberspace that regularly conduct extensive seminars and produce substantial papers on or inspired by Rand's work.

None of this suggests, however, that Ayn Rand will have made a lasting impact on our world, even on the philosophical trends that are to come. It is certain that she was an iconoclast who acted quite courageously and largely, though by no means unfailingly, abided by her own ethics in her fight for her ideas.[25]

Of course, identifying a contemporary thinker as an iconoclast is problematic. One's own era isn't so clearly characterizable as to make certain who is or who is not truly in tune with it. In addition, in choosing a given person for consideration when that person isn't hailed by one's culture, the author reveals his own esteem or respect for that person. The charge often follows that objective treatment of the person is impossible.

Yet to think this way, to deny objectivity when it is coupled with respect or even admiration, is to confuse objectivity with neutrality or nonpartisanship. A doctor needn't be neutral about a patient's ailment in order to be objective in assessing it, and deciding what treatment it requires. Even a research scientist may have a very strong interest in finding a cure for a disease and precisely for that reason adhere to strict standards of objectivity. And, furthermore, even a devoted fan of a baseball team could make a fair and objective umpire.

The problem of lacking objectivity may indeed exist for the weak-willed, for those who would easily yield to impulses or even likes or dislikes instead of making a careful appraisal. Indeed, slipshod treatment of a favorite subject can result from eagerness to paint the beautiful picture. Nevertheless, there is no necessity about being careless, so there is no necessity to subjectivity. Of course, there are pitfalls when studying someone one admires, since often the admiration tends to run ahead of the justification for it. But it is not impossible to remain objective although it requires discipline.

In the above introductory discussion I have been focusing on sketching some of Ayn Rand's contributions to various traditional branches of philosophy. A detailed analysis and evaluation of some of her work follows.

As a novelist/philosopher Ayn Rand was a unique figure in our culture. As someone who has produced a system of ideas that makes sense of areas of human life which have been all but given up as incomprehensible, she has also been exceptional and certainly iconoclastic.

Endnotes

1   She was not an (intrinsicist) realist about universals or the natures of beings, as Plato is supposed to have been. Ideas or abstractions have no separate existence, are not "out there." They—or at least valid ones—are, however, formed by the human mind in accordance with objective facts that are all particular, concrete. In value theory her "objectivism" means that goodness is a demonstrable relationship between something and that which it is good for.

2   Richard Rorty, *Objectivity, Relativism, and Truth* (Cambridge: Cambridge University Press, 1991), p. 12.

[3] W. G. Maclagan, "Self and Others: A Defense of Altruism," *Philosophical Quarterly*, Vol. 4 (1954): 109-110. Rand is often faulted for getting altruism wrong—it doesn't mean something as excessively other-directed, it is often said, as she contends. But Maclagan, who wanted to get it right in terms of the teachings of mid-century Anglo-Saxon moral philosophy, puts it exactly as Rand had done, in one of the premier philosophy journals of the time.

[4] A sympathetic character in Graham Greene's *Looser Takes All* illustrates the phenomenon when he says, "None of us has a right to forget anyone. Except ourselves." (Baltimore, MD: Penguin, 1993), p. 51.

[5] Aristotle, *Nicomachean Ethics* (1168b25-1169a8)

[6] Of course, once formal theology and even religion begin to color common sense, a different view begins to come to the fore.

[7] Ayn Rand, *Atlas Shrugged* (New York: Random House, 1957), p. 1015.

[8] Ibid.

[9] Rand herself believed that since thinking is impossible without it being produced by conceptually conscious beings, and since it is a normative activity—one can do it right or wrong but it ought to be done right—it clearly implies free will. Her argument is in *Atlas Shrugged* (New York: Random House, 1957). See my own discussion in "Applied Ethics and Free Will," *Journal of Applied Philosophy*, Vol. 10 (1993), pp. 59-72.

[10] But see Steve Rose, *Lifelines: Biology Beyond Determinism* (London: Oxford University Press, 1998), wherein the author embraces both a process concept of the human individual—a lifeline—and the idea that human beings possess free will.

[11] Ayn Rand, *Introduction to Objectivist Epistemology, Expanded Second Edition* (New York: NAL Books, 1990), p. 15. Rand states here that "The first concepts man forms are concepts of entities—since entities are the only primary existents. (Attributes cannot exist by themselves, they are merely the characteristics of entities; motions are motions of entities; relationships are relationships among entities.)" Rand here accepts Aristotle's view that beings are basic, while processes, events, relations are always derivative. A powerful challenge to this is provided in Randall R. Dipert's "The Mathematical Structure of the World: The World as Graph," *The Journal of Philosophy*, Vol. 94 (July 1997), pp. 329-74. It is not clear, though, whether Dipert's thesis, that the most fundamental elements of the world are relations, implies that Rand is wrong in taking entities to be primary.

[12] *Reliabilist* theories in our day would not fit this characterization, although they are recent arrival on the scene. J. Roger Lee called my attention to this fact.

[13] Ayn Rand, *Introduction to Objectivist Epistemology, Expanded Second Edition* (New York: Meridian, 1990), p. 1.

[14] Ibid., p. 46.

[15] Ibid., p. 85.

[16] Robert Mayhew, ed., *Ayn Rand's Marginalia* (New Milford, CT: Second Renaissance Books, 1995), p. 77.

[17] This may suggest to some that Rand rejects Aristotle's idea that one should not seek the same precision in all the disciplines. In fact, Rand would seem to

agree: The standard of precision will be different, depending on the field in question.

18   In Rand's vocabulary the concept "interest" means something different from what it has meant in the Hobbesian and economic social-science vocabulary. For Rand the issue is benefiting oneself in the broadest sense, one might say: *flourishing as a human being*. Egoism doesn't ordinarily mean this for most people, although Rand's point was to call attention to how much—even if not exclusive—attention to one's own life a sound conception of morality requires.

19   Some who are very sympathetic with her ethics—for example, J. Roger Lee, Douglas B. Rasmussen and Douglas J. Den Uyl—prefer eudaemonism or the ethics of human flourishing, so as to avoid any association with the subjectivist-atomistic version most philosophers have in mind when they use the term "egoism." Other use "ethical individualism" to mean what is essentially the same position—see, for example, David L. Norton, *Personal Destinies, A Philosophy of Ethical Individualism* (Princeton, NJ: Princeton University Press, 1976). Erin Mack, in contrast, prefers ethical egoism!

20   Hobbes, who advanced such a psychological egoist view, referred to his system of preferred human behavior as a morality, yet also denied free will and took part in numerous debates championing mechanical materialism and determinism.

21   Rand, *Atlas Shrugged*, p. 986.

22   For the distinction between natural right and natural rights, see Leo Strauss, *Natural Right and History* (Chicago: University of Chicago Press, 1953).

23   Rand eschews the term "libertarian" because she considers it unwise to divorce politics from the rest of philosophy, as many vocal libertarians prefer to do.

24   Louis Torres and Michelle Kamhi, *What Art Is: The Esthetic Theory of Ayn Rand* (Chicago: Open Court Publishing Co., Inc., 1999). This work was forthcoming during the writing of the present book.

25   The precise nature of a philosopher's impact upon or importance to us is itself a serious philosophical topic. When Hegel states that "the Owl of Minerva flies at dawn," he is suggesting that the philosopher comes into the picture with hindsight—a point that led Marx to exclaim that "philosophers have thus far only interpreted the world, the point, however, is to change it."

Rand often asserted her own superior ethical standing and morally unblemished record. Yet she was often cruel and callous toward innocent students who asked her questions in public forums and then endured unkind thrashings by Rand and her epigone. She also treated some of the greatest minds in human history with disdain—Plato, Hume, Kant (about whom more later). For a fine account of Ayn Rand's personal life, see Barbara Branden, *The Passion of Ayn Rand* (Garden City, NY: Doubleday, 1986). See also, for an illuminating and self-conscious depiction of a fictional rendition of a Randian archetype, the late Kay Nolte Smith, *Elegy for a Soprano* (New York: Villard Books, 1985).

Chapter 2:
Rand on Axiomatic Concepts

The first duty of intelligent men is the restatement of the obvious.

George Orwell

What Kind of Foundationalism?

In Ayn Rand's philosophy a central place is occupied by axiomatic concepts; roughly, ideas that we cannot do without anywhere, any time.[1] They are basic because they mean a fact that is ubiquitous, omnipresent.

What follows is an exposition of this core element of Ayn Rand's form of philosophical foundationalism, namely her "axiomatic" concepts of existence, identity, and consciousness.[2] I shall proceed in five steps. First I shall set out Rand's axioms, focusing mainly on her axiom of existence which, once spelled out as a proposition, states: "Existence exists." Next I shall discuss the nature and function of such linguistically curious expressions as "Existence exists." In section three, I shall explicate Rand's method of validating these axioms by focusing on Aristotle's defense of the Principle of Non-Contradiction. Aristotle's and Rand's approaches are similar, and Aristotle's ideas on this topic have been widely contested on a number of different grounds, so reviewing Aristotle's position will shed light on Rand's. Fourth, I will consider the kind of "evidence" we may have for the propositions that Rand and Aristotle regard as identifying basic facts, giving special consideration to the role that self-knowledge plays in providing such evidence. Last, I shall consider some contemporary objections to the Aristotelian/Randian approach.

This will not be a comprehensive treatment of axiomatic concepts but it will serve as a good start for coming to grips with an element of Objectivism that is central and has also received a good deal of ridicule. As one author wrote, "A=A. Big deal."[3] If one can make a good case that Rand's position is at least as strong as Aristotle's, such ridicule will have been significantly rebuffed.

Rand clearly thought of herself as a foundationalist. She illustrates the structure of knowledge and the relationship of philosophy to the sciences and culture with the metaphors of buildings (foundation /superstructure), armies (general/private), and trees (soil/roots /trunk/branches/leaves/fruit).[4] Indeed, Rand and those who have been developing her thought since her death seem to be simultaneously committed both to rationalist foundationalism, which seeks foundations in the broadest, most abstract principles — and to empiricist foundationalism, which seeks foundations in sensed or perceived particulars.[5]

This tendency toward dual foundationalism is amplified in the writings of her followers. Passages such as the following are common throughout her work. In support of the rationalist interpretation, we find: "Philosophy studies the fundamental nature of existence, of man, and of man's relationship to existence. As against the special sciences, which deal only with particular aspects, philosophy deals with those aspects of the universe that pertain to everything that exists. In the realm of cognition, the special sciences are the trees, but philosophy is the soil which makes the forest possible." (*Philosophy: Who Needs It?* [Indianapolis, IN: Bobbs-Merril, Co., Inc., 1982], p. 2 [henceforth *PW*). In support of the empiricist approach, in turn, we find quotes of this tenor:

> Nothing is self-evident except the material of sensory perception. (*PW*, p. 15)
>
> Man's senses are his only direct cognitive contact with reality and, therefore, his only source of information. Without sensory evidence there can be no concepts; without concepts there can be no language; there can be no knowledge and no science. (*PW*, p. 108)

Second, Rand is clearly committed to the view that all individual and cultural phenomena can meaningfully be expressed by way of knowledge claims. In other words, what human affairs is all about may be stated explicitly. And these statements then can be adjudicated by philosophy. So the facts of human affairs may be subjected to philosophical scrutiny.

This view gives rise to Rand's philosophical interpretation of history. All of history, cultural and individual, is the concrete manifestation of basic philosophical premises. The historical process is driven forward by the motor of an internal dialectic: the clash between Platonism and Aristotelianism. Although Chris Sciabarra has argued that the substance of Rand's political and cultural commentary is far more subtle and multi-dimensional than her explicit theory of history, at the hands of less attentive minds her theory of history comes off as simply a one-dimensional idealism in which all other factors are determined "in the last instance" by philosophical factors.[6] The following quotes are representative:

> The foundation of any culture, the source responsible for all of its manifestations, is its philosophy. (*The Voice of Reason* [New York: New American Library, 1988], p. 104)
>
> Just as man's actions are preceded and determined by some form of idea in his mind, so a society's existential conditions are preceded and determined by the ascendancy of a certain philosophy among those whose job is to deal with ideas. The events of any given period of history are the results of the thinking of the preceding period. (*For the New Intellectual* [henceforth *FNI*] [New York: Random House, 1961], p. 27)
>
> Philosophy is a necessity for a rational being: philosophy is the foundation of science, the organizer of man's mind, the programmer of his subconscious, the selector of his values. (*PW*, p. 99)
>
> The men who are not interested in philosophy need it most urgently: they are most helplessly in its power.
>
> The men who are not interested in philosophy absorb its principles from the cultural atmosphere around them—from schools, colleges, books, magazines, newspapers, movies, television, etc. Who sets the tone of a culture? A small handful of men: the philosophers. Others follow their lead, either by conviction or default. (*PW*, p. 8)
>
> The power that determines the establishment, the changes, the evolution, and the destruction of social systems is philosophy. The role of chance, accident, or tradition, in this context, is the same as their role in the life of an individual: their power stands in inverse ratio to the power of a culture's (or an individual's) philosophical equipment, and grows as philosophy collapses. It is, therefore, by reference to philosophy that a social system has to be defined and evaluated. (*Capitalism: The Unknown Ideal* [New York: New American Library, 1966], p. 12)

Now, while there is an enormous intellectual distance to be traversed from these sweeping, ambitious statements to Rand's narrower, more technical discussions of axiomatic concepts, she clearly believed that she had bridged this gap. Unfortunately, no attempt to trace this line of reasoning can be made here. However, since any foundationalism is only as good as its foundations, an examination of Rand's philosophical axioms is an important first step toward understanding her overall project and assessing its viability.

Rand's Philosophical Axioms

According to Rand, "*Existence exists.* (This is a way of translating into the form of a proposition, and thus into the form of an axiom, the primary fact which is existence)." (*Introduction to Objectivist Epistemology* [New York: NAL Books, 1990], p. 3-4 [henceforth *IOE*) "But," Rand goes on to add, "explicit propositions as such are not primaries; they are made of concepts. The base of man's knowledge—of all other concepts, all axioms, propositions and thought—of axiomatic concepts" (*IOE*, p. 73, emphasis added). It is axiomatic concepts that serve as the first principles of Rand's philosophy. She defines an axiomatic concept as:

> ...the identification of a primary fact of reality, which cannot be analyzed, i.e., reduced to other facts or broken into component parts. It is implicit in all facts and all knowledge. It is the fundamentally given and directly perceived or experienced, which requires no proof or explanation, but on which all proofs and explanations rest. (*IOE*, p. 55)

This would appear to square with common sense: we learn what there is, not statements or propositions about what there is, first and foremost. And while a good deal of later learning occurs via propositions—human communication—the experiences we have provide us with facts we access by means of our perceptual organs and minds.[7]

It might be objected that the relevant syntax requires that in the sentence "It is a fact that x," "x" must itself stand for a sentence or proposition, not for a concept. Rand would reply that such a view takes the understanding of facts—indeed, its expression in propositional form—as being prior to the awareness of it. One may, for example, encounter a loud bang, be aware of it, then report that one has heard a loud bang, even observe that it is a fact that it was a loud bang. But all this *follows* the presence and encounter of the loud bang;

thus the report and observation, which would both take the propositional form, wouldn't be primary.

At this point, it should be made clear in just what way Rand's axiomatic concepts are axiomatic. Put plainly, first, they are concepts that figure in all awareness, ones that are indispensable for any and all awareness. Once these concepts are understood to be basic and primary, they can be stated explicitly. But we aren't aware of them in their explicit propositional form.

In the Aristotelian tradition, two kinds of first principles exist. The first consists of basic statements describing the contents of a particular realm of phenomena that is the subject of scientific investigation. An example from geometry would be any basic definition, such as that of a point or line. These first principles are particular to specific sciences.

The second kind of first principle applies to all sciences across the board. These principles do not provide the content of the science; rather, they rule its form. These are the principles of reasoning, such as the Principle of Non-Contradiction and its corollaries, or the principle that equals added to equals yield equals. These principles are axioms. These axioms are not stated as the premises of scientific demonstrations. Rather, they identify the unspoken assumptions or presuppositions that rule and guide scientific demonstration itself (see Aristotle, *Metaphysics*, Gamma 3, 1005a19-34).

Rand's axiomatic concepts are axiomatic in this second sense. They do not appear as the premises of scientific demonstrations. Instead they (1) delimit the realm in which demonstration takes place and (2) provide the foundation for the rules of logic logical inference. That is to say, they are akin to the standards of basic measurement — e.g., the meter or the yard — that cannot be questioned. "How long is a meter?" makes no sense. "Why should one accept reality?" also makes no sense.[8]

Axiomatic concepts do not refer to the specific content of our knowledge, but to the form that our knowledge must take. The chief difference some might stress between Rand's and Aristotle's axioms is that Aristotle appears to speak explicitly of axioms solely in the context of scientific demonstration, which proceeds by deduction. Rand extends the context of axioms by pointing out that they are presupposed and grounded in inductive reasoning as well. Yet if one

understands Aristotle's principles of being as axioms, then this supposed difference disappears.

Rand's three "first and primary" axiomatic concepts are "existence," "identity," and "consciousness" (*IOE*, p. 55). "Existence"
identifies the fact that something exists. "Identity" identifies the fact
that something exists. And "consciousness" identifies the fact and
that we are aware of these other facts. By "existence," Rand means
not only what goes by the name of the "external world," but also
consciousness and its states. By "consciousness" she means "the faculty of perceiving that which exists" (*FNI*, p. 152). Consciousness is
by nature intentional: every act of consciousness is outward directed,
related to and resting upon something that exists independent of that
act.

By "identity" she means the particular, determinate natures of
that which exists. To be is to be something, to have a specific, finite
set of characteristics and potentialities. "Identity" is roughly equivalent to "nature." To say that things "have" identities is to say that
they "have" natures. But this talk of "having" natures is too loose.
Things do not so much have natures; they are natures. There is no
ghostly substratum that receives the identity of things as pincushions
receive pins. "Existence and identity are not attributes of existents;
they are the existents" (*IOE*, p. 56). Or, more succinctly: "Existence is
identity" (*FNI*, p. 152).

What motivates the identification and conceptualization of the
primary facts of existence, identity, and consciousness? The motivation is foundational: to ground human knowledge, to serve as a
guardian against error and a corrective for it. As Rand puts it,
"[A]xiomatic concepts are the products of an epistemological need—
the need of a volitional, conceptual consciousness which is capable of
error and doubt.... It is only man's consciousness, a consciousness capable of conceptual errors, that needs special identification of the directly given...." (*IOE*, pp. 58-59) This identification of the directly
given serves to "found" knowledge. But it does not do so in any conventionally "foundationalist" way.

Rand's talk of "axioms" that serve as the "base of man's knowledge—of all other concepts, all axioms, propositions and thought"
inevitably calls to mind the project of the rationalist foundationalists:
the discovery of an indubitable master axiom, such as the Cartesian

cogito, upon the basis of which we can validate all other knowledge through the use of strict logical deduction. Rand's characterization of axiomatic concepts as identifying "basic facts" of reality and "the directly given" calls to mind the empiricist foundationalist project of identifying "incorrigible" sensory or perceptual data upon which we can found all knowledge through induction.[9]

But Rand's approach is neither rationalist nor empiricist. Unlike the empiricist, whose basic facts are sensed or perceived particulars, Rand's basic facts are extraordinarily abstract and general. Existence, identity, and consciousness are simply not on the same level of abstraction as this-here patch of red or this-here tomato.

The role of Rand's axioms does not place her in the rationalist camp either, despite some similarity between Rand's concept of consciousness and the Cartesian cogito. Descartes claimed to discover the cogito as his starting point by examining his ideas until he found one that is rationally undeniable. Rand, however, holds that we learn axioms from experience. It is only after we have apprehended or grasped the axioms, in the course of our contact with the world by means of sensory experience, that we can go on to show that they are rationally undeniable.

Whereas the rationalists claim that we can supply—or at least validate—the content of our knowledge by pure logical deduction from self-evident, innate truths (for which no experience of reality is required—nor could be invoked, since it is the veracity or validity of such experience that is in need of showing), Rand does not see knowledge as having to be deduced from axioms—although she does talk about their "corollaries." This would make what she—or anyone else, of course—concludes depend upon a conceptual rather than pure logical inference. (We will turn shortly to the difference between pure formal deductions and conceptual inferences and derivations.)

In explaining how her axioms serve as the framework of knowledge proper, Rand actually drops the metaphor of building upon foundations, employing instead the metaphor of "guidelines" for an activity or game, and the metaphor of enframing, embracing, enclosing, or delimiting a space or field:

> It is only man's consciousness, a consciousness capable of conceptual errors, that needs special identification of the directly given, to embrace and delimit the entire field of its awareness—to delimit it from the void of unre-

ality to which conceptual errors can lead. Axiomatic concepts are epistemological guidelines. They sum up the essence of all human cognition: something exists of which I am conscious: I must discover its identity. (*IOE*, pp. 58-59, emphasis added)

Rand makes it clear that she is only surveying and staking out the site upon which human knowledge is built. The edifice of knowledge rests upon experience, not upon philosophical axioms. To tinker with the metaphor, the axioms may serve as the cornerstones of the structure, but not its foundations. Her axioms provide only the most general form of knowledge, not its specific content—the widest frame, not the individual brushstrokes:

The concept "existence" does not indicate what existents it subsumes: it merely underscores the primary fact that they exist. The concept "identity" does not indicate the particular natures of the existents it subsumes: it merely underscores the primary fact that they are what they are. The concept "consciousness" does not indicate what existents one is conscious of: it merely underscores the primary fact that one is conscious. (*IOE*, p. 59)

Rand's axiomatic concepts—perhaps one of the most widely misrepresented elements of her thinking, competing only with her ethical egoism for this honor—delimit the form of knowledge in two general ways. First, they lay down the boundaries of possible experience. Whatever in fact we happen to experience, it will exist—i.e., it will be other than the conscious act which is our experience of it. Thus we can simply ignore the solipsists who claim that conscious acts create their objects *ex nihilo*. Furthermore, whatever we happen to experience, it will "have" an identity—i.e., it will be determinate. Thus we can ignore those who claim that they have experienced something that is both red and green (i.e., not-red) at the same time and in the same respect. And finally, whatever we happen to experience, it will be an experience—i.e., we will be conscious in experiencing it.

Thus we can smile bemused at those psychologists and philosophers who claim that they are aware of data that indicate consciousness, intentionality, and the given are myths. Here, too, Rand is in a very small minority among contemporary philosophers, especially those, like Richard Rorty, who are center stage in our culture.

The second way in which Rand's axioms delimit the form of our knowledge is well captured by her metaphor of "guidelines." The axiomatic concept of identity, when stated in propositional form is "A is A," the law of identity, which along with its corollaries, is the foundation of logic.

Although Rand treats experience rather than philosophical axioms as the foundation of knowledge, this does not imply that she is in any conventional sense an empirical foundationalist. There are two main reasons for this.

First, Rand rejected and tried to distance herself from what is conventionally called empiricism—and, by extension, from empiricist forms of foundationalism. Consider the following, written in 1970:

> For the past several decades, the dominant fashion among academic philosophers was empiricism—a militant kind of empiricism. Its exponents dismissed philosophical problems by declaring that fundamental concepts—such as existence, entity, identity, reality—are meaningless; they declared that concepts are arbitrary social conventions and that only sense data, "unprocessed" by conceptualization, represent a valid or "scientific" form of knowledge; and they debated such issues as whether a man may claim with certainty that he perceives a tomato or only a patch of red. (PW, p. 100)

The essential point here—never mind for now that Rand is nearly caricaturing such thinkers—is Rand's rejection of the empiricist idea of a "unprocessed" sensory "given." Rand holds that this radical empiricism is but the flip side of the rationalist view that we can know simply by the manipulation of concepts without relation to sensory evidence: "Accepting empiricism's basic premise that concepts have no necessary relation to sense data, a new breed of rationalists...declar[es] that scientific knowledge does not require any sense data at all (which means: that man does not need his sense organs)" (PW, p. 101).

Rand, however, holds that all knowledge is based on the evidence of the senses and that all perceptual knowledge is processed. "All knowledge is processed knowledge—whether on the sensory, perceptual or conceptual level. An 'unprocessed' knowledge would be a knowledge acquired without means of cognition" (IOE, p. 81).[10]

Now to the second, and most fundamental, reason why Rand is not an empiricist foundationalist. Foundationalism of both the rationalist and empiricist varieties arises from what Richard J. Bernstein has called "Cartesian anxiety."[11] Cartesian anxiety itself arises from entertaining the possibility that mind and reality can be totally separate—that the truth of the entirety of our knowledge can meaningfully be called into doubt—that all of our common sense knowledge can be suspended in "scare quotes" and treated as "mere beliefs," which then have to be justified by establishing their representational relationship with the external world. In other words, Cartesian anxiety arises from the idea that consciousness may in fact not be conscious of something other than itself, that all we know may in fact be floating ideas composed out of the stuff of consciousness and internal to it. Once this radically skeptical possibility is raised, it is simply optional whether we argue our way out to the external world on the basis of rationalist principles or empiricist sense data.

Rand is not this kind of foundationalist because she does not suffer from Cartesian anxiety. For Rand, consciousness is conscious of something. This does not mean that in the task of identifying what we are conscious of, we are infallible. But it does mean that we are in conscious contact with reality. Rand is well aware that doubt, uncertainty, error, illusion, "mere appearances," "mere opinions," and other privations of consciousness can and do occur. But these can be identified as such only within the context of there being something of which I am aware and that I might identify or misidentify later when I get to it. If there were nothing of which I was aware, there would be no prospect of my being wrong about it in my (non-existent) conscious awareness of it.[12]

Once the search for knowledge commences, the methods of the special sciences are the standards by which we judge something to be a mere appearance, a mere opinion, an error, and so forth. Such knowledge is the background against which we can identify doubt, uncertainty, and illusion. Anything else Rand would charge with the commission of "the fallacy of the stolen concept," namely, the concept that arises from scientific inquiry.

Rand wards off skepticism by showing that existence is axiomatic. For example, how could one proceed to say anything true enough about the matter of our capacity to know or fail to know reality if one rejects Rand's view that existence is axiomatic? How could the skeptic know that fact—that we cannot know reality—if beliefs can just hang out there, detached from reality? What could ever render such skeptical views themselves true?[13]

In other words, it is plainly arbitrary for the skeptic to "blow up" or expand opinion, error, and uncertainty to encompass all of our knowledge.[14] Surely there is something illegitimate about taking a pair of mutually defining correlatives—such as knowledge/opinion or appearance/reality—and then suppressing one term while totalizing the other. In what sense, then, would "appearance" still mean appearance when its correlative, reality, is suppressed? If the skeptic no longer has the background of knowledge against which to identify mere opinion, then what evidence can he offer for his knowledge that there may be no knowledge and only mere opinion? If the skeptic no longer has the standard of knowledge against which he can judge something to be erroneous, then what evidence can he give us that we might always be in error? The answer is: The skeptic can't offer good reasons. Hence the Cartesian hypothesis that an evil demon may be deceiving us; hence the serious contemporary philosophical discussions of brains in vats that believe (do brains believe?) they are walking, talking human beings. And the result of these rather paranoid fantasies is Cartesian anxiety.

Rand is not a conventional foundationalist because she simply doesn't let the whole modern foundationalist project get off the ground. But this does not mean that Rand should be identified with contemporary anti-foundationalist philosophers. Most of these philosophers are simply frustrated foundationalists. They accept the legitimacy of the entire modern philosophical project—then they simply deny that there are any solutions. Rand does not simply deny the solutions. She denies the problem as well.

Rand's Use of Language

The identification of existence, identity, and consciousness is not "informative," if informative speech is arbitrarily restricted to the production of "synthetic" propositions. Nor is it informative in the sense of communicating something surprising and novel. Everyone knows these facts, or can know them upon a moment's reflection. As soon as they are stated, it seems less as if they have imparted new information than reminded us of something that we have known all along. The purpose of identifying them explicitly is, again, not so much to inform as to underscore—the basic framework of human cognition. This underscoring is reflected in the formal axioms drawn from these concepts. Axiomatic concepts can be transformed only into repetitive or "tautologous" axioms, such as "Existence exists—Consciousness is conscious—A is A" (*IOE*, p. 59).

To dismiss these axioms with the claim that they are repetitive, banal, or obvious is simply to miss the point. Of course they are obvious. If they weren't they wouldn't be identifying basic facts. Rand takes philosophy with the utmost seriousness. Its purpose is not to titillate with novelty but to contemplate and appreciate eternal verity. Given this conception of philosophy, repetition is not an impoverished mode of speech, but the highest and deepest. Repetition, moreover, is especially necessary in the current intellectual climate. Rand, like Orwell, thinks that our culture has sunk to such a level of skeptical decadence that it is necessary to identify, repeat, and defend the obvious.

To put this in somewhat metaphorical terms: A normal subject-predicate proposition has a certain inner structural tendency, a tug or flow toward the manifold and particular. When the subject term is set down, reference to some phenomenon is established: "Cat." Then, through predication, the phenomenon can be articulated internally—"The cat is a noble beast"—or related "outward" to other things in the world—"The cat is on the mat." Aristotle tells us that a proposition is a *ti kata tinos legein*—something said of something. In Greek, the preposition "kata" has the sense of "emanating out from something and down upon something else." The flow of a proposition is all "downstream," toward greater articulation, manifoldness, and plurality. Viewed from the perspective and anticipations set up by propositional thinking, the use of tautology and repetition, by throwing thought backward toward its subject, thus seems like an abortion of thinking. But, in fact, it is a call to a new thinking—thinking that reverses thought's natural "downstream" momentum, carries it upstream to its source, and then tries to grasp that source: subject, substance, *ousia*.

The same essential movement can take place on the predicative level of thinking, i.e., the taking of something as something. Instead of predicating p as S, we can take S as p—and we can take ourselves backward to appreciate S as S. For instance, we can investigate being as moving, being as living, being as countable, being as thinking—or simply being as being.

Besides Aristotle two other thinkers' ideas of metaphysical language are similar to Rand's: Hegel and Heidegger.

In Hegel's system, the rough equivalent of a proposition like "Existence exists" is what is called the "speculative proposition" (der spekulative Satz). The speculative proposition is best understood in contradistinction to what Hegel calls the "understanding." For our purposes, the understanding is the kind of mentality that reads propositions in a distanced and highly discursive manner, following and therefore anticipating the propositional tug from subject to predicate, and the argumentative tug from proposition to proposition, searching always for specifics, for facts, and for conclusions. By contrast, the speculative sentence demands a different kind of thinking. Hegel puts it this way:

> Here thinking, instead of making progress in the transition from subject to predicate, in reality feels itself checked by the loss of the subject, and, missing it, is thrown back on the thought of the subject. Or, since the predicate itself has been expressed as a subject, as the being or essence which exhausts the nature of the subject, thinking finds the subject immediately in the predicate; and, now, having returned into itself in the predicate, instead of being in a position where it has freedom for argument, it is still absorbed in the content, or at least faced with the demand that it should be .... This abnormal inhibition of thought is in large measure the source of the complaints regarding the unintelligibility of philosophical writings from individuals who otherwise possess the educational requirements for understanding them. Here we see the reason behind one particular complaint so often made against them: that so much has to be read over and over before it can be understood—a complaint whose burden is presumed to be quite outrageous. ...It is clear from the above what this amounts to. The philosophical proposition, since it is a proposition, leads one to believe that the usual subject-predicate relation obtains, as well as the usual attitude toward knowing. But the philosophical content destroys this attitude and this opinion. We learn by experience that we meant something other than what we meant to mean; and this correction of our meaning compels our knowing to go back to the proposition, and to understand it in some other way.[15]

As for Heidegger, he, like Rand herself, is interested in tracing out, articulating, or distinguishing the most fundamental concepts,

and recognizes that this task can be accomplished only in unusual—
i.e. repetitive and tautological—language. Heidegger, furthermore,
recognizes the underscoring rather than informative nature of such
utterances. Consider, for example, this passage from *What Is Called
Thinking?*:

> Language is not a tool. Language is not this and that, is not something else
> besides itself. Language is language. Statements of this kind have the prop-
> erty that they say nothing and yet bind thinking to its subject matter with
> supreme conclusiveness.[16]

Consider also Rand's "Existence exists" alongside such much-
ridiculed Heideggerisms as "Appropriation appropriates," "the
Nothing annihilates" "the thing things," and "the world worlds."[17]

Rand and Aristotle

Now we turn to the method by which Rand grasps these primary
facts, conceptualizes them, and defends them. Rand offers the following test for the axiomatic nature of a concept. There is a way to
ascertain whether a given concept is axiomatic or not: one ascertains
it by observing the fact that an axiomatic concept cannot be escaped,
that it is implicit in all knowledge, that it has to be accepted and used
even in the process of any attempt to deny it (*IOE*, p. 79).

Rand sets this out as a method by which we can ascertain whether
a concept is axiomatic or not, but it is not and cannot be a means of
directly and logically proving that a concept is axiomatic, for axiomatic concepts identify basic metaphysical conditions that must hold
before any proof can take place, thus rendering any direct proof circular. For instance, the attempt to prove that something exists presupposes the existence of a prover. The attempt to prove the existence
of consciousness is itself an act of consciousness. The attempt to
prove the existence of identity or determinateness is itself governed
by the Law of Identity.

But although this method does not directly prove Rand's metaphysical axioms, it does allow an indirect proof resembling both the
reductio ad absurdum and the argument from the elimination of all
other possibilities. This is the method of demonstration by refutation.
By venturing the denial of any basic metaphysical fact, it can be

shown that all alternatives to accepting such facts are incoherent. One simply points out that axiomatic concepts identify facts which ground the possibility of all thought, including any attempt to demonstrate them—or to deny them. For instance, the denial of existence presupposes the existence of a denier. The denial of identity involves acts of cognitive distinction, which would be impossible in a world without particular, determinate identities. The denial of the existence of consciousness purports to be consciousness of a fact and requires the actions of a conscious subject.

The type of error made in attempting to deny these facts is not merely the logical contradiction found between two inconsistent statements. It is a more fundamental, metaphysical "contradiction" between an action and the ground of the possibility of that action.

Now such reasoning almost always strikes philosophers as somehow fishy, but it does have a long history and a venerable origin. To my knowledge, its earliest occurrence is in Socrates' response to Protagoras in Plato's *Theatetus* (170a-171d). It seems to arise most prominently, however, in Aristotle's *Metaphysics*, book Gamma, chapters 3-8, where Aristotle sets out and defends the Principle of Non-Contradiction (henceforth the PNC).

Aristotle does not state precisely why the PNC is one of those things that is not subject to demonstration, but the reason is plain enough: one must employ the PNC in all reasoning; therefore, any attempt to prove the PNC is by necessity circular. Even when some attempt to circumvent this fact, they run afoul of the attempt since in offering their denials, they themselves must deploy concrete facts, words, letters, and so forth, that must be what they are just in order for the denial *to be a denial*. If the denial were true, it would be both a denial and not a denial and thus would have no identity and couldn't be identified successfully for what the proponents would like it to be identified.

Aristotle's next step is to discuss those who deny the PNC. Aristotle distinguishes between two forms of the denial of the PNC. The first form might be termed the honest form. Some thinkers, in earnestly working through philosophical problems, happen to come to conclusions which implicitly or explicitly deny the PNC. "Those who come to such belief [i.e., the denial of the PNC] from the difficulties they have raised can easily be cured of their ignorance; for our replies will be directed not to their vocal statements but to their thought" (1009a17-20). These thinkers can be corrected simply by examining their reasoning and introducing helpful distinctions, such as actuality and potentiality. (See 1009a31-35.) Also, if the denial of PNC were true, it would be both a denial and not a denial and thus would have no identity and couldn't be identified successfully for what the proponents would like it to be identified.

The other form of denying the PNC can be termed dishonest or contentious. In responding to such denials, one does not seek to address the thoughts of the denier, but instead focuses on his words: "those who state such a doctrine for its own sake can be cured by a refutation of that doctrine as expressed in speech and in words" (1009a20-22). Aristotle describes the logic of demonstration by refutation thus:

> That the position of these thinkers [e.g., those who deny the PNC] is impossible can also be demonstrated by refutation, if only our opponent says something. ... Demonstration by refutation...differs from demonstration in this: that he who demonstrates might seem to be begging the question, but if the other party is the cause of something posited, we would have a refutation but not a demonstration. The principle for all such arguments is not to demand that our opponent say something is or is not (for one might believe this to be a begging of the question), but that what he says should at least mean something to him as well as to another. (1006a12-22)

Thus far, the tactic is clear. Any attempt to directly prove the PNC is circular. But any attempt to deny it renders the denier guilty of a self-referential inconsistency. Once this inconsistency is committed, then the defender of the PNC need only point out the hopelessness of the opponent's position.

But how, precisely, does this work? An obvious story would be: First the skeptic offers an argument concluding with the denial of the PNC. Then one simply points out that all arguments are ruled by the PNC; therefore, such an argument presupposes what it denies, i.e., it is self-referentially inconsistent. But this is not Aristotle's strategy. Aristotle does not hold that it is necessary to deny the PNC *per se* in order to open oneself to demonstration by refutation. Nor does he hold that one's denial has to take the form of an argument. Instead, Aristotle claims that what is denied is difference. He holds, furthermore, that the denial of difference can be shown to be self-refuting on three levels: (1) speech, (2) indication without speaking (e.g., pointing or shrugging), and (3) action. Note that argument per se does not appear on this list. Aristotle holds, furthermore, that there is a state of being in which the denial of the PNC does not open one to demonstration by refutation: a purely passive, vegetative existence. I shall treat each of these matters in turn.

Aristotle's extended arguments throughout chapters 4 to 8 are haunted by two specters: Eleatic monism and the Heraclitean flux. Eleatic monism is the affirmation of identity to the exclusion of difference, and the affirmation of stasis to the exclusion of change. The Heraclitean flux is the affirmation of difference to the exclusion of identity, and the affirmation of change to the exclusion of stasis. Aristotle holds that both positions are identical insofar as they exclude the possibility of meaningful speech: For the Eleatic monist, only one thing can truly be said of being: that it is. Anything more than this tautologous registration of sameness would introduce distinction, which requires the existence of non-being, which is impossible. For the Heraclitean Cratylus, all beings are in such a state of flux that he "criticized even Heraclitus for saying that one cannot step into the same river twice, for he himself thought that one could not do so even once" (1010a13-15). If everything is totally different, then each thing is different from itself, i.e., there is no identity; nothing is anything; everything is nothing. This to say that total difference (non-identity) leads us to total indifference: everything is the same (i.e., completely different, even from itself), an ineffable and unspeakable situation which reduces Cratylus the Heraclitean to Eleatic reticence: "Cratylus finally thought that nothing should be spoken but only moved his finger" (1010a12-13).

By contrast, Aristotle, like Plato in the *Sophist* (254d-259d) and elsewhere, holds that identity and difference are equally primordial and irreducible to one another, something Rand would contest on grounds that identity must be prior. Aristotle's point perhaps is mirrored by the fact that for him the three highest principles of logic—Identity, Non-Contradiction, and Excluded-Middle—are corollaries, neither derivable from nor reducible to one another. Aristotle thus holds that the denial of the PNC can be refuted if the skeptic simply affirms the identification of the difference. But this cannot be the affirmation of difference *simpliciter*. In order to be distinguished from the indifferent difference of Cratylus, the affirmation of difference must be against the backdrop of the affirmation of identity.

The affirmation of identity and difference takes place in speech. Thus when the skeptic denies the PNC, one can refute him by pointing to the fact that he does indeed deny the PNC (identity) and not something else (difference). If the skeptic is truly contentious and, infuriated by the attempt to refute him on the grounds of speech, retreats into silent gesturing, one can again point to the fact that he gestures here (identity) and not there (difference). Indeed, this determinateness is what allows us to distinguish a meaningful gesture from a mere involuntary reflex. If the skeptic persists in his denial and turns to stomp off in a huff, one can point out, as Aristotle does, that:

> It is most evident that no one of those who posit this doctrine, or anyone else, is disposed in his actions in the same way. For why does a man walk to Megara and not stay where he is with the thought that he is walking to Megara? And why does he not walk straight into a well or over a precipice, if such happens to be in his way, but appears to guard himself against it, with the thought that it is not equally good and not good to fall in? Clearly he believes one course of action to be better [identity] and the opposite not better [difference]. (1008b12-19)

If the skeptic chooses to pursue his denial further, there is only one resort: to sit down, shut up, and cease to function cognitively. But even this does not yield victory in argument. Or if it does, it is a pyretic victory. "That the position of these thinkers is impossible can...be demonstrated by refutation, if only our opponent says something; and if he says nothing, it is ridiculous to seek an argument against one who has no argument insofar as he has no argument, for such a man qua such is indeed like a vegetable" (1006a12-16).

This, then, is Aristotle's treatment of the PNC. We are now in the position to evaluate it. The first and most salient conclusion is the undeniable persuasive power of Aristotle's approach. But in virtue of what is it persuasive? Precisely what kind of argument is it? To this question I now turn.

Self-Knowledge

Arguments are commonly divided into inductive and deductive forms. Aristotle's demonstration of the PNC by refutation is not a deductive argument, direct or indirect, for it is precisely the foundation of deduction that is in question. It must, therefore, be a form of induction. But we must be careful here. The PNC is somehow drawn from experience and then validated by showing the self-referential inconsistency of its denial. But this is not, however, a standard enumerative form of induction, for the PNC does not purport to apply only to observed particulars. Nor is it open to falsification by newly observed particulars. Rather, the PNC makes its claim about all beings—actual or possible, universal or particular, observed or unobserved: Whatever ultimately is, it is what it is, and it is not what it is not at the same time and in the same respect. The PNC, then, seems to occupy a realm between deduction and enumerative induction. This realm, I contend, is best seen as the realm of reflection. As Rand puts it:

> Axiomatic concepts identify what is merely implicit in the consciousness of an infant .... (Implicit knowledge is passively held material which, to be grasped, requires a special focus and process of consciousness. ...) (*IOE*, p. 57)

But what is this special "act of the intellect," this "special focus and process of consciousness"? What it is isn't clear. It is not a process of inductive generalization. We do not go around enumerating things, saying "This exists, and this exists, and this exists; therefore, existence exists." Nor is it a process of abstracting differences. Existence is not the ineffable residue that is left over once one boils off all determinations. Rather, one moves from "My linguistic capacity exists; it is what it is, and I know it" to "There is something; whatever it is, it is what it is, and I know it" in two steps.

First, there is a reflective turn, a step back from directly knowing things, to reflectively knowing the knowing itself. Second, there is a shift in focus from the content of our knowledge to its form. This is not achieved step by step, by a process of progressive abstraction. Rather, it happens in a single stroke, by a process that can be called "formalization." One simply zaps out the content or determinations of the experience, leaving a formal scheme, "existence-identity-consciousness" into which any particular content can be plugged.

Rand's metaphysical axioms are, therefore, wholly formal in both origin and intent. They originate through reflection upon and formalization of the nature of experience. And, once they are derived, they serve as a permanent, neutral formal framework for knowledge, the material content of which is to be provided by empirical inquiry. Rand puts it thus:

> Axiomatic concepts are epistemological guidelines. They sum up the essence of all human cognition: something exists of which I am conscious; I must discover its identity. (*IOE*, p. 59)

There are two salient virtues of this "formal" foundationalism. First, it is extremely austere, compact, and minimalist. It places only three basic constraints on empirical inquiry, leaving all questions of content, and more specific questions of form or method, open to be debated by scientists and other inquirers who have expertise with the phenomena in question. This leads to the second virtue. Through its formal austerity and minimalism, Rand's axiomatic foundationalism escapes from both the problems of modern foundationalism and the problems of modern anti-foundationalism.

Anti-foundationalists, for example, are quite right to criticize what can be called "armchair" philosophy: the pretense on the part of many philosophers to investigate the particulars of the world, or to determine the specifics of scientific method, by a priori means, without dirtying themselves with any actual hands-on experience. We all know the types: the modern Pythagoreans deducing the existence of modern "counter-Earths": particles or forces that simply must exist to satisfy their latest philosophical theories. Or the modern verification experts who, on the basis of dated popular science books, decide how the sciences must proceed if they are to discover the truth.

Rand's approach, by contrast, is so minimalistic and open-ended that she seemed uninterested — at least qua philosophical researcher — with even such traditional philosophical questions as the ontological status of fictions. (Whatever they are, they simply are what they are.) Rand's approach is also consistent with a healthy respect for the primacy of scientific practice, an open-minded ontological pluralism, and an (almost) anything goes, (almost) Feyerabendian laissez-faire attitude toward the methods of factual investigation. The questions of the method and content of inquiry are left to the experts, to those who have something interesting to say about them: the investigators themselves.

Foundationalists, however, are correct to point out that anti-foundationalists will involve themselves in self-referential inconsistencies. For instance, Feyerabend's methodological anarchism, if carried out consistently, is self-negating. After all, if no methodological option can be ruled out in advance by philosophical means, then methodological dogmatism is just as much an option as methodological pluralism. It may just be the case that tomorrow a rigid form of dogmatism might "work." Rand's formal minimalism, however, can serve both as the foundation of pluralism and prevent pluralism from negating itself. It founds pluralism by delimiting the form, rather than by determining the content and method of inquiry. It preserves pluralism by formally eliminating the possibility of contents or methods which foreclose the open-ended form of knowledge. In short, whereas Feyerabend's unlimited anarchism is subject to an internal dialectic that makes it ultimately self-negating, Rand secures pluralism from self-negation precisely by limiting it under the minimal government of her axiomatic concepts.

The Virtue of Axioms

To conclude, I believe that I have established that Rand's axiomatic foundationalism has a number of philosophical virtues. It is a highly economical and original recovery and development of central threads of the Aristotelian tradition, standing outside of both the rationalist and empiricist tendencies of modern epistemology. Indeed, to the extent that modern epistemology is premised upon treating solipsism as a conceivable possibility and therefore the problem of the external world as a live issue, Rand's foundationalism can be characterized as post-epistemological, even post-modern—yet not post-philosophical and post-rational.

Another virtue of Rand's project is its systematic ambitiousness. The sketchy outline above is, in fact, an outline of a defense of human reason and the prospect for guiding us to understanding reality and to the possibility of success in leading a truly human life. Both of these prospects are under severe attack, with serious consequences for both the profession of philosophy and for human life.

Rand's Objectivism, of all the schools of contemporary philosophy, may well be the one that holds out the best, most reasonable, hope for completing and validating the Enlightenment project of creating a society that is both rational and intellectually responsible on the one hand, and free and pluralistic on the other. This society is one in which the open-ended inquiries of the sciences, the arts, and the other participants in the conversation of humankind can take place, not in spite of a foundationalist philosophy, but precisely because of a minimalist foundationalism—uncovers those conditions and limits that make free and rational inquiry possible in the first place.[18]

It is also possible that what Rand has done is to avoid the Enlightenment's major error, namely, to deny morality as such—as distinct from some perverse version of it—a naturalist normative base. Rand sketches what amounts to a full-fledged position of the accessibility to reason of the most perplexing aspects of human life, namely, its normative dimensions.

It is to this project we turn next.

Endnotes

[1] It bears mentioning that an idea (according to Rand) is a relational or intentional aspect of the mind, so to speak connecting consciousness with the world in a way that's hard to explain because it is unique to human life, as it were, *sui generis*. Clearly, however, concepts or ideas are not entities or beings "in" the mind, as, say, the cerebral cortex is in the brain. In a sense ideas are doings or acts of the human mind.

[2] Rand's primary treatment of her axiomatic concepts is in chapter 6, "Axiomatic Concepts," in her monograph *Introduction to Objectivist Epistemology*.

Henceforth, in the present chapter, I shall cite Rand's works in the body of the text, not in the notes. Since the pagination of the hard bound and paperback versions of Rand's works varies, I shall adopt the convention of citing the hard bound versions' pages.

It is worth noting here that Ayn Rand often writes as if her foundationalism held that all aspects of science, history, culture, and so forth. can either be reduced to philosophical influences or should be reduced to them by being philosophically criticized and reconstructed on "firm foundations." This view emerges from reading Rand on philosophy in Harry Binswanger, ed., *The Ayn Rand Lexicon* (New York: New American Library, 1986), pp. 358-362.

In this discussion I am not treating Rand as this sort of foundationalist but rather as a foundationalist vis-à-vis the current debate between Richard Rorty and his critics. Here the foundationalist holds that the foundations in questions are formal or transcendental by articulating the nature and limits of reality and, thus, also our reasoning about it, namely, the delimitations or demarcations of the different realms of scientific, historical, artistic, and other forms of life. For criticism of such foundationalism, though without reference to or appreciation of Rand's minimalist versions, see Richard Rorty, *Philosophy and the Mirror of Nature* (Princeton, NJ: Princeton University Press, 1979), and *Objectivity, Relativism, and Truth* (London: Cambridge University Press, 1991). (Incidentally, Rorty is very likely aware of some of Rand's philosophical work, having been the dissertation guide to David Kelley when the latter wrote his *The Evidence of the Senses: A Realist Theory of Perception* [Baton Rouge: Louisiana State University Press, 1986].)

3   Leon Wieseltier, *Against Identity* (New York: William Drenttel, 1996), p. 57. Interestingly, Wieseltier's book accords on many points with Rand's social and political views, given its criticism of the collectivist ideas involved in ethnicity and cultural identity. In ethics, however, Wieseltier seems to champion altruism: "...[S]elflessness does not mean that you do not have yourself or that you do not know yourself. It means that you have been drawn out of yourself. It is the self-denial of the strong" (p. 70). For Rand this portrays a very impoverished notion of the human self. She would hold that properly understood, the right kind of outreach is selfish to the core, because the self is very much, albeit critically, engaged with the world, including others (who deserve its care and attention). Surely Wieseltier wouldn't hold that one ought to be drawn out of oneself for just any purpose, at the beck and call of anyone (Hitler, Mussolini?). But if there are to be terms of engagement, whose terms are they to be if not the agent's? It is personal integrity, a well-cultivated human soul, which enables one to navigate all the requests for one's support. And that, for Rand, is selfishness *par excellence*. See, also, Nathaniel Branden, *Honoring the Self* (New York: Bantam Books, Inc., 1985).

4   See Ayn Rand, *Philosophy: Who Needs It* (New York: Bobbs-Merrill, 1982), pp. 99, 10, 13-14.

5   See, for example, Leonard Peikoff, "Knowledge as Hierarchical," *The Objectivist Forum* 7 (December 1976), pp. 1-11. Throughout this essay, Peikoff repeats that the foundation of knowledge lies in perceived particulars. He then ends his essay by saying that, "If your reduction [of concepts to their basis in 'sense data'] is accurate, you will find that that base is the axiom with which we began: existence exists." (p. 11)

6   See Chris Sciabarra, "Ayn Rand's Critique of Ideology," *Reason Papers* 14 (Spring 1989), pp. 32-44.

7   This is a point developed in great detail in Edward Pols, *Radical Realism, Direct Knowing in Philosophy and Science* (Ithaca, NY: Cornell University Press, 1998).

54

8   We may note that this lines Rand up with those who consider the question, "Why is there something rather than nothing?" nonsensical. The reason? One is expected to escape reality—which is everything at all—in order to give an account of it, to explain it. But that is impossible—reality is all there is. This issue is worked out in great detail in Edward Pols, *Radical Realism, Direct Knowing in Science and Philosophy* (Ithaca, NY: Cornell University Press, 1992).

9   Aristotle states that it is the task of the philosopher to investigate all beings insofar as they have being, and "to examine also the principles of the syllogism" (1005b8), which are not only logical, but also ontological principles: "the most certain principles of all things" (1005b12, emphasis added). Such a principle (or principles) must be "that about which it is impossible to think falsely," "most known," and "non-hypothetical" (1005b14-15). The reason for this is, Aristotle says, that it is "a principle which one must have if he is to understand any thing." It is something "which one must know If he is to know anything," and thus it "must be in his possession for every occasion" (1005b15-18).

It is in this spirit, I believe, that Rand's often ridiculed axioms must be taken, although, of course, much dispute exists on just exactly how Aristotle himself saw the matter (e.g., on what exactly "a principle which one must have" means).

10   David Kelley—in his *The Evidence of the Senses*; "A Theory of Abstraction," *Cognition and Brain Theory* 7 (1984), pp. 329-357; and an exchange with Peter Munz, a reviewer of *The Evidence of the Senses*, in *Critical Review* vol. 2, no. 4 (Fall 1988), pp. 183-7—aligns himself with the empiricist tradition. Consider the following.

Professor Munz ("Sense Perception and the Reality of the World," [*Critical Review,*] Winter 1988) is correct in placing my work in the tradition of empiricists who hold that perception is the basis of our knowledge of the world, the foundation of any certainty we may achieve. My approach differs from that of other empiricists in many respects, including the one that he mentions: I regard perception as a distinct mode of cognition, intermediate between sensations on the one hand and conceptual knowledge on the other. Unlike sensation, perception is the awareness of entities: stable objects in three-dimensional space. Unlike conceptual knowledge, this awareness is direct, it involves no interpretation, and can therefore serve as a non-circular cognitive ground for conceptual knowledge of those objects (p. 183, emphasis added).

Rand says that "A percept is a group of sensations automatically retained and integrated by the brain of a living organism. ...The knowledge of sensations as components of percepts is not direct, it is acquired by man much later: it is a scientific, *conceptual* discovery" (*IOE*, p. 5). It is evident, then, that according to her the empiricist thesis that what we know first of all is sensations or sense-impressions is wrong. On the other hand, she is an empiricist in the sense that Kelly declares himself one, namely, that the constituent elements of what we know first of all, percepts, are sensations.

11 Richard J. Bernstein, *Beyond Objectivism and Relativism: Science, Hermeneutics, and Praxis* (Philadelphia: University of Pennsylvania Press, 1983).

12 I thank J. Roger Lee for the formulation of this point.

13 It would be an interesting study to compared Rand's approach to skepticism and knowledge and that presented in Ludwig Wittgenstein's last book, *On Certainty* (Oxford: Basil Blackwell, 1969).

14 For a discussion of the "blow up" fallacy see Tibor R. Machan, *The Pseudo-Science of B. F. Skinner* (New Rochelle, NY: Arlington House, Publishing Company, Inc., 1974).

15 G. W. F. Hegel, *The Phenomenology of Spirit*, A. V. Miller trans. (Oxford: Oxford University Press, 1977), pp. 38-9.

16 Martin Heidegger, *What Is Called Thinking?*, trans. J. Glenn Gray and Fred D. Weick (New York: Harper and Row, 1968), p. 153.

17 Martin Heidegger, "Time and Being," in *On Time and Being*, Joan Stambaugh, trans. (New York: Harper and Row, 1972); "What Is Metaphysics?," David Farrell Krell, trans., in *Basic Writings*, David Farrell Krell, ed. (New York: Harper and Row, 1977), p. 105; and "The Thing," in *Poetry, Language, Thought*, Albert Hofstadter, ed. and trans. (New York: Harper and Row, 1971).

18 I received a great deal of help from Gregory R. Johnson, especially, as well as from Roger Bissell, and J. Roger Lee in the development and composition of this chapter.

Chapter 3:
Rand's Moral Philosophy

The Objectivist Meta-ethics

This chapter will concentrate on Ayn Rand's way of justifying ethics and on clarifying what her ethical egoism comes to.

Meta-ethics is that part of epistemology that pertains to the issue of whether and how we can know what is right and wrong and whether *ethical* or *moral* knowledge exists. Rand supported cognitivism—the contention that such knowledge is possible. Once she became confident in this position, she proceeded to lay out her version of the ethics of egoism, the view that the purpose of ethics is to secure one's happiness as a human being.

Rand starts her investigations into ethics by noting that "The first question that has to be answered, as a precondition of any attempt to define, to judge or to accept any specific system of ethics, is: *Why* does man need a code of values?"[1] She adds, "In ethics, one must begin by asking, What are *values*? Why does man need them?"[2]

For Rand ethics exists so as to guide us to a successful life as human individuals. "What ... are the right goals for man to pursue? What are the values his survival requires? That is the question to be answered by the science of *ethics*. And *this* is why man needs a code of ethics. ...Ethics is an objective, metaphysical necessity of man's survival—not by the grace of the supernatural nor of your neighbor nor of your whim, but by the grace of reality and the nature of life."[3]

If it is true that the nature of human life is such that values are indispensable, this will establish that values have a cognitive status, just as they do in, for example, the more specialized sciences of nutrition or medicine. Both of these disciplines deal with values. When a diet or medication is prescribed, these prescriptions are grounded in facts, including the fact that some things are better for people's well-being than others. So in these fields it is understood that one can discover what values are, what is good and what is bad for people's physical health. Rand argues that the same is true when it comes to their overall well being. Of course, this presupposes that living as a human being is what consistent actions are aimed at, just as medical values presuppose that health is what consistent medical actions are aimed at. But Rand would respond to those who consider this a kind of subjectivism—one might have chosen something else, after all, than living—that ethics is irrelevant to those who chose death. "The standard of value of the Objectivist ethics—the standard by which one judges what is good or evil—is man's life, or: that which is required for man's survival qua man."[4] And, to quote Rand's protagonist John Galt, who speaks for her on these and other matters, "There is only one fundamental alternative in the universe: existence or nonexistence— and it pertains to a single class of entities: to living organism."[5] Which is to say that for human beings who must make choices to guide themselves, the basic choice is to live or not to live, to exist or not to exist. Once that choice to live is made, consistency demands that they judge and conduct themselves by the right code of ethics for the kind of living entity they are, rational animals.

Rand, incidentally, is unique among classical liberals—those who champion that social-political philosophy in terms of which communities must embrace the principle of individual (negative) rights to life, liberty, and property—in that she believes that statements with moral import are capable of being shown to be true or false. Randian individualism isn't of the subjectivist sort one hears so much about when economists talk of and detractors criticize the American political system of capitalism. (Rand is also unique in that she explicitly defends the idea of free will, albeit briefly and mainly via the works of Nathaniel Branden.[6])

Classical liberals have tended, in the main, to embrace the position that moral "judgments" are not judgments but rather expressions of preferences for and against various things. Rand believed, instead, that we can ascertain whether such judgments are true. She held that ethics is within the cognitive sphere, an aspect of reality that is capable of being understood. As she puts it, "An organism's life is its *standard of value*: that which furthers its life is the *good*, that which threatens it is the *evil*."[7]

How could Rand forge ahead this way, unabashedly producing moral claims, when she was aware that doubts about the cognitive status of ethics have loomed large, especially via the famous "is-ought" gap or, what later came to be called, the naturalistic fallacy?[8] These doubts have undermined the confidence of several generations of highly influential philosophers in the possibility to rest ethics on anything solid at all. So why not Rand's?

To appreciate Ayn Rand's contribution to moral philosophy, let us take a look at her way of treating these skeptical challenges.

The Challenge from the Humean Skeptic

The "is-ought" gap expresses the philosophical claim that a conclusion that contains moral terms such as "ought to" or "ought not to" cannot be *deduced* from premises that lack those moral terms because valid deductive arguments can only have in their conclusions components that are fully supported by its premises. If the premises fail to support the conclusion, the conclusion is not valid. Here is how Hume put the point:

> ...In every system of morality which I have hitherto met with, I have always remarked, that the author proceeds for some time in the ordinary way of reasoning, and establishes the being of a God, or makes observations concerning human affairs; when all of a sudden I am surprised to find, that instead of the usually copulation of propositions, *is*, and *is not*, I meet with no proposition that is not connected with an *ought*, or *ought not*. This change is imperceptible; but is, however, of the last consequence. For as this *ought*, or *ought not*, expresses some new relation or affirmation, it is necessary that is should be observed and explained; and at the same time that a reason should be given, for what seems altogether inconceivable, how this new relation can be a deduction from others, which are entirely different from it....[9]

Hume discredits all rationalist efforts to prove moral judgments true. He does this by arguing that they beg the question because such a proof would have to have premises that already contain the crucial term, *ought* or *ought not*, thus simply pushing the problem back a step in each case, leaving the moral judgment ultimately unprovable.

Rand says to this that "It purports to mean that ethical propositions cannot be derived from factual propositions—or that knowledge of that which is cannot logically give man any knowledge of what he ought to do. And wider: it means that knowledge of reality is irrelevant to the actions of a living entity and that any relation between the two is 'inconceivable.'"[10]

Of course, Hume complained about trying to *deduce* ought and ought not from is or is not. A deduction is deemed by many philosophers to be a formal logical operation, capable of involving only concepts with closed, final definitions. They treat deductions as timeless proofs.

When logic is deployed to produce proofs involving facts that may imply other facts, this is not, for most of them, a deduction but some other type of proof—another way to *derive* a factual proposition from others. Hume didn't discuss the difference and we shall see that Rand's Objectivist epistemology holds out a credible promise for the success of such a derivation but does not establish that the strict formal deduction Hume thinks is inconceivable is actually available in establishing or proving moral propositions.[11]

In any case, Hume's view about the basis of ethical claims has made an enormous impact on the social sciences and moral philosophy. By affirming what to many appeared as an unbridgeable gap between factual and value judgments, it laid the foundation for positivism. This is the view that while what are called empirical facts are something we can know about, values are not within the province of the knowable.

A major reason the social sciences have mostly kept away from making value judgments is that they invoke the "is-ought" gap, saying, "Therefore handling values would be unscientific, inaccessible to factual confirmation." Since the hard sciences had been closely associated with the idea that factual judgments can be confirmed, the social sciences, to carry "the mantle of science," were fashioned to mimic them. The method by which the evidence and reasoning of the hard sciences is supposed to proceed—data gathering and unbiased analysis—needed to be followed and this precluded dealing with values, including morality and politics.

Rand, not unlike many other philosophers, didn't take into account the distinction between Hume's claiming we cannot *deduce* moral conclusions and the possibility of deriving them in some other way from factual premises. She took the former claim to affirm the impossibility of rational moral judgments, thus showing a tendency toward rationalism, even though in her epistemological works she disavowed it.

Moore's Naturalistic Fallacy Challenge

G. E. Moore argued that no definition of "goodness" or "value" can succeed because they can all be questioned. Moore says, "Or if I am asked, 'How is good to be defined?' my answer is that it cannot be defined, and that is all I have to say about it." The most famous reason Moore gave is what is called the open question argument. As he put it,

[I]f, for example, whatever is called 'good' seems to be pleasant, the proposition 'Pleasure is the good' does not assert a connection between two different notions but involves only one, that of pleasure, which is easily recognized as a distinct entity. But whoever will attentively consider with himself what is actually before his mind when he asks that question 'Is pleasure (or whatever it may be) after all good?' can easily satisfy himself that he is not merely wondering whether pleasure is pleasant. And if he will try this experiment with each suggested definition in succession, he may become expert enough to recognize that in every case he has before his mind a unique object, with regard to the connection of which with any other object, a distinct question may be asked. Every one does in fact understand the question 'Is this good?' When he thinks of it, his state of mind is different from what it would be, were he asked 'Is this pleasant, or desired, or approved?'[12]

What this comes to is that Moore thinks a definition is a necessary truth, so that when one states "Goodness is X," the question, "Is goodness really X?" cannot make sense, any more than it would make sense to ask about a triangle whether it really has three angles. Because, he argues, we can meaningfully ask, "Is goodness really X?" that must mean that goodness cannot be defined at all.

Randian Responses to Hume's Skeptic

As I suggested above, it is the Randian epistemologist who could best respond to Hume by reminding him that in fact we have very few deductive arguments we make about anything, so he hasn't made a very big point after all—only against radical rationalist ethics. Science (medicine, physics, chemistry) and technology (engineering, forensic science are not based on deductive arguments. Very little, indeed, in our cognitive apparatus rests on deduction. Such argumentation is the province of pure, formal logic and some parts of mathematics (such as Euclidean geometry).

Now it is true enough that Hume's use of "deduce" was not technical and thus what he advanced was not simply the limited and true idea that one cannot deduce moral conclusions from factual premises. Instead he seems clearly to have believed that factual premises cannot contain moral elements—the *is* for Hume appears to be unable to contain value, as when we speak of something *being* good. This would follow from Hume's empiricist epistemology: knowledge of facts is always knowledge of sensory impressions, no more.

Hume's conception of facts is unique. It certainly does not reflect what we mean by "facts," as in "the fact is that Johnny has an excellent car," "the fact is not in dispute, Jeffrey Dahmer was a vicious murderer." The fact of Johnny's excellent car, let alone of Johnny's own excellence, has no place in Hume's worldview because, well, excellence cannot be ascertained through the apprehension of mere sensory impressions. Nor is there any fact about murder since the concept has a moral component, namely, wrongful killing, and "wrongfulness" is not perceivable in Hume's empiricist epistemology.

In the Randian metaphysics, however, facts aren't barren as they must be in Hume's. The Randian epistemology opens the possibility of one's knowing facts not merely as bits of data by way of sensory impressions but as beings of a certain kind that are known via rational identification. The other reason is that metaphysical facts are evident to any thinking entity and need not be constructed from sensory input.

For Rand, much of human knowledge is the result of a process that consists of reasoning that amounts to conceptual development. It can either be argued that the logic here is different from pure deduction or that a sense of "deduction" as in "derivation" is clearly not inconceivable here because the premises of the relevant arguments will contain value terms as parts of the identification of something. Rand makes this note in her journals which illustrates the point: "Man exists and must survive as a man."[13] She calls this an axiom, a basic, undeniable fact. It can be ascertained to be one but not via empiricist epistemology. It can be learned, ascertained, even verified or confirmed but not solely by means of sensory impressions. One learns it by paying attention with all of one's faculties of awareness—perceptual and rational. Many may not learn it at all, in part because they do not choose to follow the conceptual development involved. This alone plays into skeptical hands, since it makes it plausible to doubt the claim, never mind how well argued it may be—it is always "logically possible," some will claim, that it is false. (Rand thinks that's nonsense.)

If we add to this another fact Rand believes we can identify, namely, that "Man's particular distinction from all other living species is the fact that his consciousness is volitional,"[14] and explicate "volitional" as "requiring the initiative of the agent for the action to take place," the conclusion emerges that "Man ought to initiate his form of consciousness." And that, in essence, is the Randian ethical egoism: *One ought to, first and foremost, think!*[15]

It is impossible to square this sort of identification of facts and derivation of ethical conclusions with Hume's strict empiricism. It is because by mere reliance upon the sense impressions, facts such as those Rand takes us to be capable of identifying cannot be identified.

Interestingly, neither do most social scientists—those who accept the implications of Hume's empiricism for the relationship between *is* and *ought*—embrace Hume's empiricism and skepticism in all areas of human knowledge. Strictly worked out, Hume's position leads to solipsism—that all we know is the insides of our minds.

In the twentieth century, some decided that it is not just ethics we know nothing about but everything else, including the hard sciences. All we can attest to is some collective beliefs, no knowledge of reality.

Rand versus Moore

Rand's view confronts Moore's by flatly rejecting the idea that "goodness" is undefinable. The reason, however, isn't simple.

It is, first of all, Moore's understanding of what a definition must be that is mistaken: It is not a necessary truth in the way, say, "p -> p" is a necessary truth of logic. Ayn Rand understood by definitions something very different.

As she explains her position, "A definition is a statement that identifies the nature of the units subsumed under a concept....The purpose of a definition is to distinguish a concept from all other concepts and thus to keep its unities differentiated from all other existents."[16] Definitions identify what many things share that makes them what they are and distinguishes them from other things. The nature of something is whatever about it makes it what it is. A definition states this fact about those beings.

Now this is not novel—definitions have been understood along these lines since Socrates. Most significant, though, is that Rand considers definitions contextual: "[A]ll conceptualization is a contextual process; the context is the entire field of a mind's awareness or knowledge at any level of its cognitive development.... *All definitions are contextual,* and a primitive definition *does not contradict* a more advanced one: the latter merely expands the former."[17]

To put it a bit differently, what a definition does is provide the best statement *to date* of what a given kind of thing is. Implicit here is the idea that knowledge is not some final picture or claim about reality but the most up-to-date identification of it. To know, then, is not to have finally, completely, fully grasped what one knows but to have grasped it as well as possible for now.

This pretty much pulls the rug from under the skeptic who has hitched his doubts to the fact that many philosophers promise knowledge to be something it isn't. Descartes is a good example of this, as is Plato. Both believed that to know must involve an understanding of something that cannot be improved upon, could never be altered, modified, revised. Ayn Rand recognizes that that is not what knowledge amounts to, akin to how the famous twentieth century British philosopher J. L. Austin did in his essay "Other Minds."[18]

Now how might Rand answer Moore's open question case against the definability of goodness?

First, definitions aren't analytic truths, formal logical propositions such as "A = df., x, y, z." Such formalized symbolizations of definitions are misleading because they present us with a wrong model of actual definitions, as if they were static, unchangeable, timeless. (We will turn to this shortly but the previous chapter sets the stage for the possibility of realistic definitions.)

Second, when one defines a concept such as "goodness," because it is not a necessary truth, it is plausible enough to ask whether the definition is in fact a good or sound or well-formed one. Since with normative concepts, definitions spell out something very controversial, no wonder people will contest any candidate.

But this is true in the sciences, as well. Certainly any novel idea's definition is going to be contested. Yet, in the hard sciences, at least, the controversy will subside because widespread motivation doesn't exist for remaining a contrarian if the case for the definition has been made well enough. In ethics, especially, this is not the case: all kinds of motives may prompt one to question even the most convincing definition. One might find that such a definition indicts one's character, one's history of conduct, one's favorite people, and so on. One may care very much about becoming complacent about what goodness is and continue to question what is advanced simply to be as sure as we can be about the matter.

In short, Moore's explanation for why one can intelligibly question the proposed definitions of "goodness" is wrong: not because "goodness" is undefinable but because even the best definition is unacceptable to those who might be disadvantaged from having it accepted.

Conceptualization versus Deduction

The idea of concept formation clarifies why Rand does not accept either Hume's or Moore's idea of what it is to know something and to define a concept. Put plainly, what is at issue here is the claim that the way we acquire knowledge is to develop and organize our ideas based on awareness we have of the world for the time being, by means of our perceptual organs, guided by axiomatic concepts (which we have already discussed). In a bit more detail, the process goes on roughly as follows:

One detects various similarities and differences by means of the sensory organs; one recognizes that nothing like that is possible unless something exists that is being perceived, and then one carefully, parsimoniously, arranges a system of ideas that observes the principles of logic as well as keeps in continued focus the initial differences and similarities, thus learning what it is that exists. The result is a system of sound—well-grounded—ideas that best (but not necessarily finally) capture for us reality.

When we know reality, moreover, we do not know by grasping it for all times. We know it at a time, not for all times. Knowing reality is not easy to spell out because it isn't like other things we are familiar with: human beings are unique in knowing as they know, so it has to be identified without analogies. But some come closer than others. We know as we might grasp something as well we can, but not without the possibility of improvement.

In any case, almost anything that we do when we draw conclusions—about whether to open a door when trying to go through it, or how to construct a bridge or build a helicopter or space ship—the conclusion is not strictly speaking deduced—as formal logicians would characterize deductions—but conceptually inferred from successive facts that are known in the fashion just characterized. Because one might learn, later, that what one knew before can be known a bit differently now, it is also possible to imagine that later it will be known differently.

The reason this is different from pure logical deduction is that such deductions are formal, symbolic and thus not dependent on actual concepts, only on symbols of concepts. As such, strictly logical deductions are timeless.

Let us look at a simple syllogism from term logic, first, then at one from propositional logic. We will see why they can mislead us about the nature of logical argumentation about substantive matters.

> All As are Bs,
> all Bs are Cs,
> so, all As are Cs,

This "argument" does not pose the problem of "A" being open ended, not *finally* identified. To put it slightly differently, the "concept of A" (unlike the concept "human being" or "apple" or "lion") looks finally closed so the argument is deductively valid. Let's consider an "argument" from propositional logic:

> $P \rightarrow Q$
> $Q \rightarrow R$
> $P \rightarrow R$

"A" (or "B" or "C") is not a concept but a symbol standing in for one. But the way the symbol behaves in formal arguments must not be confused with how concepts would. Nor are "P," "Q," and "R" propositions—they simply stand in for them. To appreciate the nature of reasoning, it is necessary to explore the nature of terms and propositions, not their symbolic representations in formal logic texts.

Compare the formal symbolic syllogism with the following: "All human beings are biological entities, all biological entities are mortal, so all human beings are mortal." The concepts here are not finally locked in, so it is "intelligible" to propose that the conclusion does not follow since the second premise might be false. The mortality of animals is not a logical truth, as one might put it in terms of contemporary analytic philosophy. But so what?

Indeed, science fiction writers create plausible enough stories by often denying various parts of this and similar syllogisms. The conclusions are, thus, not formally valid unless one settles on a statement of what an animal or biological entity is, one that may not be the last word on the subject. But then some will argue the definitions merely stipulate, not confirm, the reality's changeable nature.

Purely formal deductive arguments have no problems like this. Which is why what is involved in most reasoning is not formally deductive but conceptual (logical) inferences, in which a very significant role is played by theories and definitions. Rand made this a central part of her epistemology.

Platonic Legacies versus Objectivism

It is Plato who set us off on a wrong course here because for him, as for Descartes later, the objective of rational inquiry appears to have been *final* knowledge, *the last word on a topic*, the *perfect form* of something.

Modeling his view on Euclidean geometry and other aspects of mathematics, Plato wanted to grasp the formal, eternal properties of things. Anything less wasn't knowledge. And Descartes reinforced this when he argued that knowledge must be certain beyond a shadow of doubt: so the denial of what one knows cannot even be imagined or conceived.

Consider: if you know your birthdate, is it really impossible that it couldn't be imagined that you are wrong? That is clearly not so; in much of what we know, it is easy to think something else is true. But according to the Platonic-Cartesian idea of what knowledge must be, we don't really, truly know these things.

Randian epistemology rejects this trap. It is the trap, incidentally, that skepticism exploits. Since such a ridiculous task—as knowing an eternal truth in each case of knowing something—is unachievable but having at hand the Platonic-Cartesian model of what knowledge must be, well then, knowledge is not possible.

Instead, the Objectivist epistemology holds that while there may be some (very few) things we know in that way—namely, basic facts of reality that make themselves evident in everything (via axioms)—many others we know in an open-ended way, with the possibility of development, alteration, or modification.

As such, reasoning in the substantive sciences, including ethics, involves concepts that are open-ended and one can always speculate on some new or modified definition for them that would alter the premises and conclusions of the argument. And in a field such as ethics, where so much controversy, disputation—not to mention culpable disingenuousness, vagueness, and ambiguity—is in evidence, taking a different position appears more plausible than in one of the hard sciences. (Indeed, the closer and closer one comes to the human situation, the less and less rigorous it appears a science becomes. But this may simply be apparent in line with too many cooks—some not even interested in preparing food—spoiling the dish!)

How Does This Affect Ethics?

We have already noticed how these epistemological considerations play an important part in Objectivist ethics.

Every science begins with theories or definitions, though often they may be hidden or suppressed. (This is not so for philosophy because in this field the first step is to figure out how we must reason in the first place, which leaves open the question whether we must have definitions for that purpose. Of course, even in philosophy we deploy implicit definitions.) In ethics, which for Rand is an exact science no less than biology or meteorology, we can do the same thing. We can develop a sound (but fairly complex) theory or definition of the good and then advance to a (somewhat more complex) theory of the moral good, although most people will not do this. Those who take on the task in earnest do this, in part, by checking whether these render our experiences in the world intelligible, sensible, practicable, consistent with all known data pertaining to the field in question; and then we move on and reason from that for our particular cases.

So Rand proceeded in ethics: from a metaethical cognitivism—that was not formally deductivist but conceptually inferential—drawing on theories and definitions that are sound beyond a reasonable doubt, concluding with the best answers to the questions faced in the area addressed by the question, "How should I act?" — that is, in what has come to be called the field of ethics or morality.

As noted already, this is not all that different from engineering. There are general principles of engineering sciences and then there are particular cases for which these principles are employed to guide — how to build bridges, hotels or gas stations and so on. The reasoning is never purely deductive, although once a sound definition or theory is at hand, one can deduce, with the aid of appropriate additional premises, ethical or political conclusions. It's always inferential. It's always conceptually developed, moving from a concept to a next concept to next concept and see whether this is the most economically sensible way to account for the environment of the phenomena around you. Here is Rand's major argument in which this emerges clearly:

> Metaphysically, life is the only phenomenon that is an end in itself: a value gained and kept by a constant process of action. Epistemologically, the concept of "value" is genetically dependent upon and derived from the antecedent concept of "life." To speak of "value" as apart from "life" is worse than a contradiction in terms. "It is only the concept of 'Life' that makes the concept 'Value' possible"[19]

Rand holds that this shows that ethics is just as much a rigorous science as, say, biology. Nonetheless, the one feature of ethics distinct from the other sciences that has caused no end of puzzle is all the disagreement and controversy we find in the field. Why, the puzzle goes, if ethics is a science, does it not produce the sort of widespread consensus we find in physics, biology, or even economics? Granted, there are controversies in those disciplines, as well. They have to do more with areas of the field where developments occur and knowledge is still provisional than with the disputes about fundamental issues we find in ethics.

The puzzle is due to several factors: For one, work in a given science is voluntary and the participants select themselves if they already want to reach conclusions based on methods of reasoning that are disciplined, rigorous, not concerned with how one feels or where one comes from. Cultural origins and such do not have a role for those who take a scientific approach to reality. A program on television is able to present a dozen or so astrophysicists, all in tune with one another, discussing the latest account of the origin of the universe. (Of course, even in the sciences there are controversies but these do not reveal basic differences in what people think but rather the lack of full development of some explanation or theory.) But when a group of ethicists meet, no end of dispute ensues—say, concerning surrogate motherhood, assisted suicide or cloning.

The second difference is that ethics involves us all, not just a select group of dedicated specialists. It includes people who don't even believe in ethics, or who have very different ideas as to what "good" and "evil," "right" and "wrong" mean. Some individuals who chime in on this topic would actually prefer to weasel out of some conception of goodness or right action, while others want to undermine the entire idea of ethics. In ethics we get input from those who raise such questions as "Why should I be moral?"[20] Whereas in biology or chemistry none of the specialists are concerned about whether biology or chemistry is a bogus field or something invented. There are people who talk like this about science but they usually do not engage in scientific work.

Ethics, in short, is not a specialty—its province is all human conduct, including the very people who might deny ethics or who would champion ethical views that are bizarre. Even though the question, "Why should I be moral?" is not really a valid question—if it means "Why should I take morality seriously in the first place?"— those who ask it get the benefit of the doubt by taking part in the philosophy's broad, Socratic method, whereby no comers are barred unless they become violent.

Still, as Rand would point out, morality is inescapable—just being human enlists all of us, who aren't crucially incapacitated and are adults, into the role of making decisions as to what one will do, decisions that can be good or bad ones.

Here all kinds of troubles arise, especially with those who make bad decisions but would like it not to matter much. There are lots of people who say, "Well, that principle of ethics or moral virtue— honesty, courage, productivity, and even rationality—is fine for you, but need it hold for me?" Variations on this theme abound—I am from a different culture, different religion, different age group, different race, etc., so the ethics you embrace is not for me. And because the conclusions as to what we ought and ought not to do are always based on non-deductive arguments, so there is always the slight (logical) possibility that they contain some slippage—a definition is not quite fully developed and can, thus, be almost reasonably contested— disagreements are profuse. Indeed, the disagreements themselves tend to carry a kind of moral tone: "How dare you suggest that you can figure out what I or we ought or ought not to do?" That this rhetorical question itself suggests some moral conclusion for us all often escapes those who ask it.

Can a cognitivist, such as Rand, make sense of all this disagreement? Can the cognitivist say, "Yes, despite all the earnest disagreements in ethics, cognitivism is still true. We can have moral knowledge. Disagreement is not decisive in showing lack of objectivity. Some ethical claims are right, others are wrong."

Can that make sense? Why should anyone not agree with a moral judgment if it's something that is true no less so—no less objectively— as something would be in the natural sciences? How can Ayn Rand and her allies on the cognitivist team handle this problem?

Rand didn't enter into the debate itself at great length—she had very little patience with skeptics in any sphere of rational inquiry.[21] But perhaps she would have agreed that part of the answer is that ethics is a highly self-referential discipline. Unlike in most of the hard and even some of the social sciences—other than perhaps psychology—in ethics when we make statements, these statements reflect on us. They characterize us. When we say, "the people ought to be honest," that judgment includes us.

Now, if we don't welcome or feel comfortable about being honest, then we don't welcome the claim that people ought to be honest, especially if honesty is supposed to mark us as acting well rather than badly. If we say that people ought to abstain from killing or stealing, being lazy bums, promiscuous or unfaithful to their spouses—if we make any kind of moral judgment like that—and if we try to be integrated about these (consistent within ourselves), then these claims can come haunting us. People can say, "But look at you. You are not being honest, faithful, diligent, etc., thus you are not up to snuff as a human being."

This is not very frequently the case with other sciences that are much more oriented toward studying things that have no bearing on human character and quality. Physics or even biology does not bear on matters that are up to us, where we are the acting agents. Psychology and sociology do, and, of course, both are beset with warring schools and explanations.[22] Those in the hard sciences, however, look at the world and try to find the order in it and leave oneself, the observer, pretty much out of the equation except as yet another entity with no regard for its merits or moral qualities.

But ethics doesn't leave the observer's worth at arms' length. Judgments in ethics bear on the one who makes those judgments: to claim that human beings ought to be honest or diligent or courageous means that the one making those claims should be also. If he is not, this reflects badly upon him. Most intellectuals, and most of us when we are in a role of the intellectual, try to get things right about the world and ourselves, and we do not welcome coming off wrongheaded. We get defensive and often may go so far as to try to obscure things rather than confess to having erred, especially if we have invested a good deal of energy in working out our position. (This, by the way, is true even in the history of the natural sciences.)

So it's much easier to understand that people would like to dodge the force of ethics, where what they conclude is so directly self-referential. They don't particularly like the idea that someone else could know they are wrong, haven't behaved well.

When one says that a person is bad or evil, that's a harsh thing to say. And when this can be diffused by skepticism, that's a soothing accomplishment. Many of those accused of a crime then toy with the defense that there is no such crime as they are accused of or that in their case at least there was no real crime committed, just a misunderstanding. Clarence Darrow was perhaps the most famous defense attorney to advance this contention (for example in his defense of Leopold and Loeb).[23]

That's at least one of the explanations why subjectivism, relativism and, more generally, noncognitivism are very appealing.

Another explanation Rand would probably embrace and has hinted at herself is the truth of individualism. In fact very few moral judgments—at least in the Randian framework—are entirely universalizable. Maybe just one or two such as "Think straight. Pay close attention. Or focus or try to understand the world." In Randian language, rationality is the one universal moral principle: Think! (In the next chapter this individualist aspect of Rand's thought will be more fully explored.)

The rest of ethics is often going to vary from person to person, depending upon their circumstances, situation, role in life, the age in which they live, and so forth. What is crucial within the Randian framework is that none of that makes them relative or subjective. Yet, some think that when you individualize and diversify morality, then morality becomes subjective. It is agent-relative, as some have noted,[24] meaning that what one ought to do or ought not to do will be guided by the agent's nature both as a member of the human species and as assuming various roles in various circumstances in life.

To think of this as relativist or subjectivist is akin to believing that just because particular engineering principles applied to different building projects will be different and not universalizable, that makes engineering (and the science on which it rests) a subjective discipline. It doesn't. It makes it a pluralistic practical discipline. It requires many, many different ways of thinking through the principles and applying them to practical problems.[25]

Rand holds that values and moral values are objective—neither intrinsic, so that the goodness of something lies within it, independent of how it relates to something else—or subjective, so that the goodness is imparted to it by one's desiring it. As Rand puts it:

> The objective theory holds that the good is neither an attribute of 'things in themselves' nor of man's emotional states, but an evaluation of the facts of reality by man's consciousness according to a rational standard of value. (Rational, in this context, means: derived from the facts of reality and validated by a process of reason.) The objective theory holds that the good is an aspect of reality in relation to man—and that it must be discovered, not invented, by man. Fundamental to an objective theory of values is the question: Of value to whom and for what?[26]

The point that the good must be discovered is crucial—it is part and parcel of its being good (for one) that it is discovered to be so by one, ergo attempts to force the good upon those not willing to embrace it are inherently impossible. "The objective theory of values is the only moral theory incompatible with rule by force."[27]

So these are the basics of Randian meta-ethics. Let me turn to some points of Rand ethical egoism (or individualism) before developing it in the next chapter.

Rational Egoism

Rand basically answers the question, '"How should I act?" by reference first and foremost to one's human nature. "How should I (a human individual) act?" And she believes, in my view, that "should" amounts to "What would make me a better person in the variety of options available to me?"

This is why hers is a naturalistic ethics. It requires some understanding of human nature. The reason Rand then identifies thinking as the good-making virtue — as the virtue that is central to human living — is that human beings are presumably distinguished in nature by their capacity and dependence upon reasoning.[28]

Now the famous Randian ethical egoism here is simple: you — your self or ego — get better and better by means of your agency if and only if you act in accord with your nature. That's the nature of Rand's egoism.

You will notice that this is not the kind of egoism that is mostly taught in elementary ethics courses where egoism means do anything that damned well happens to please you. That is a form of egoism that doesn't even exist in the history of philosophy. It exists in a crude type of psychology — because of its and other social sciences' scientism — nobody really advocates it as an ethics. As I've noted before, I call Rand's a *classical* egoism or individualism. It's not the doctrine that everybody is always selfish. It's not the doctrine that says: "Do whatever you want to do." It is the doctrine that the way to become good at human life is to be a thinking, reasoning, attention-paying person.

I think to have made these contributions to ethics (or to moral philosophy) alone warrants considering someone of philosophical significance. Whether it also warrants considering her a worthy thinker is a topic for another discussion.

Endnotes

1   Ayn Rand, "The Objectivist Ethics," in *The Virtue of Selfishness* (New York: New American Library, 1974), pp. 13-14.
2   Ibid., p. 16.
3   Ibid., pp. 22-23.
4   Ibid., p. 23.
5   Ibid., p. 15.

6   Nathaniel Branden, *The Psychology of Self-Esteem* (New York: Bantam Books, 1969). For Rand's own brief defense, see Galt's Speech in *Atlas Shrugged*. Subsequent to both of these works some who have been inspired by Rand have taken up the task of defending free will. See, Stephen Boydstun, "Volitional Synopses, Parts I and II," *Objectivity*, Vol. 2, Nos. 1 & 2pp. 109-138; pp. 105-129. See, also, Tibor R. Machan, *The Pseudo-Science of B. F. Skinner* (New Rochelle, NY: Arlington House, 1973).

7   Ibid., p. 17.

8   The first is associated with the work of David Hume, whereas the latter with that of G. E. Moore.

9   David Hume, *A Treatise of Human Nature*, Garden City, NY: Doubleday & Company, Inc., 1961), p. 423.

10   David Harriman, ed., *Journals of Ayn Rand* (New York: Dutton, 1997), p. 863.

11   Rand can be interpreted as holding that the kind of strictly formal deductions others think exclusively deserve the term are simply very broad, *symbolic models* of logical reasoning. So she would argue that deductions do, in fact, obtain between judgments of facts involving concepts that are themselves contextually—as distinct from timelessly—defined, possessing essential attributes that make logical deductions possible. So her objection to Hume is that Hume failed to see that concepts such as "ought to" and "ought not to" can be derived from definitions of "human goodness" as, in part, essentially involving choices and ultimate values. In other words, Rand would argue that a sound, valid theory of human goodness deductively yields moral conclusions, what one ought to do, so long as by "deduction" is not meant logical arguments involving closed definitions of concepts.

12   G. E. Moore, *Principia Ethica* (Buffalo, NY: Prometheus Books, 1988), pp. 16-17.

13   Op. cit., *Journals of Ayn Rand*, p. 304.

14   Ibid., pp. 19-20.

15   In *Atlas Shrugged* Galt puts it this way: "If I were to speak your kind of language, I would say that man's only moral commandment is: Though shalt think. But a 'moral commandment' is a contradiction in terms. The moral is the chosen, not the forced; the understood, not the obeyed. The moral is the rational, and reason accepts no commandments" (p. 944). Whether this is a form of ethical egoism is itself in dispute. Yet, Rand here, like others elsewhere, offers her a version of a standard school of ethics. In her view what makes the Objectivist ethics a form of egoism is that it by way of practicing the virtues that one achieve one's flourishing in life, one's survival *qua* human being. In other words, one's ultimate good as a human individual depends upon acting ethically.

16   Ayn Rand, *Introduction to Objectivist Epistemology* (New York: Meridian Books, 1990), p. 40.

17   Ibid., p. 43. It is interesting that despite Rand's reputation as some kind of absolutist, she makes ample room for classifications that are not fully determinate. "In the case of existents whose characteristics are equally balanced between

the referents of two different concepts—such as primitive organisms, or the transitional shades of a color continuum—there is no cognitive necessity classify them under either (or any) concept. The choice is optional: one may designate them as a sub-category of either concept, or (in the case of a continuum) one may draw approximate divining lines (on the principle of "no more than x and no less than y"), or one may identify them *descriptively*—as the nominalists are doing when they present the "problem" (pp. 73-4). Rand also makes it clear that definitions are contextually but not "changelessly absolute." (p. 47)

18   J. L. Austin, *Philosophical Papers* (Oxford: Clarendon Press, 1961), pp. 44-84.

19   Op. cit., *The Virtue of Selfishness*, p. 18. Compare with Karl Popper: "I think that values enter the world with life; and if there is life without consciousness (as I think there may well be, even in animals and man, for there appears to be such a thing as dreamless sleep) then, I suggest, there will also be objective values, even without consciousness." Karl Popper, *Unending Quest* (Glasgow: Fontana/Collins, 1974), p. 194.

20   Kai Nielsen, "Is 'Why Should I be Moral?' an Absurdity?" in Rosalind Ekman, ed., *Readings in the Problems of Ethics* (New York: Charles Scribner & Sons, 1965), pp. 357-364. Nielsen's argument completely depends upon the use of the dubious notion of logical possibility. He notes, against someone with whom he is arguing about the matter, "I will not deny that this is nonsense of a kind: but it is not logical nonsense....[W]e have no right to reject contexts like the above. ...as unintelligible or logically absurd. We can, however, as logicians, point out their esoteric nature. But it does not deductively follow that because they are esoteric we must grade them down" (p. 363). This is noted against those who would argue that it is impossible to reject morality, to absent oneself from moral involvement, to be outside the moral game, as it were. The reason? It is that, though the idea is esoteric, it is not logically absurd. Which means, it does not involve a formal contradiction such as p->p or p^-p. "Intelligible" means no more than that— the way what science fiction writers often present is intelligible.

Of course, such intelligibility requires suspension of disbelief, ridding one's mind of knowledge that would conflict with the supposition at hand. This is just the sort of epistemological maneuver that Rand considered philosophically unsound.

21   Moreover, Rand discussed her critics in distinctly polemical tones, besmirching them as she spoke to their points. She notes, for example, concerning Wittgenstein's idea that definitions should be understood on the model of family resemblances: "[This] theory...is a perfect description of the state of a mind out of focus" (*IOE*, p. 78).

22   Not to mention disputes as to whether they are bogus. See, Thomas S. Szasz, *The Myth of Mental Illness* (New York: Harper & Row, 1961), as a classic challenge to the very legitimacy of much of what passes for the medical sciences of psychology and psychiatry.

23   Clarence Darrow, "A Plea in Defense of Loeb and Leopold," in Ekman, *Readings*, pp. 260-264.

24 Both Douglas J. Den Uyl and Eric Mack have discussed this feature of ethics.

25 An interesting alternative to Rand's ethics is Avrum Stroll's Wittgensteinian view that because there is no clear definition of the concept "human being" — that is, the use of the concept does not admit of some constant features—"we cannot do what the model implies we can always do, namely, make infallible assessments about the rights or wrongness of an act per se or about the conduct of those who participate in it." So, no foundation for ethics exists, by this account. Avrum Stoll, "Ethics without Principles," in K. S. Johannessen and T. Nordenstam, eds., Wittgenstein and the Philosophy of Culture (Vienna: Holder-Pichler-Tempsky, 1996), p. 311. Rand would reply, however, that there is a contextually true definition of the concept "human being" and it provides a basic principle for ethics, namely, rationality. Indeed, when Stroll illustrates how his ethics without principles works, what is clear is that he reasons out whether some conduct—a certain variety of incest—is ethically sound.

26 Ayn Rand, *Capitalism: The Unknown Ideal* (New York: New American Library, 1967), in "What Is Capitalism?" p. 22.

27 Ibid., p. 23.

28 It is worth noting here that Rand's secular naturalism has been subjected to much disdain, even ridicule, mainly because of the prominence of either secular conventionalism or theological naturalism. Her realism about natures—as evident in her discussion of definitions and what they are about ("definitions must identify the *nature* of the units, i.e., the *essential* characteristics without which the units would not be the kind of existents they are") in her *Introduction to Objectivist Epistemology* (p. 42)—is now echoed in what has come to be called the "naturalized epistemology" movement. See, for example, Hilary Kornblith, *Inductive Inference and Its Natural Ground* (Cambridge, MA: MIT Press, 1993).

Chapter 4:
Rand's Rational Individualism

Individualism Improved

In all of the history of moral and political thought, it is Ayn Rand who spelled out the tenets of a new, improved individualism or egoism. Rand took up this mission because she didn't believe the American political tradition of individual rights had a solid enough defense and because she thought this position, which she thought could be fully justified from more basic philosophical ideas, provides it with such a defense. How successful is the product of her work?[1]

Individualism is the social-political idea that in human community life, the human individual is most important. This is because every human being is in some irreducible way an individual, first and foremost. Clearly human beings are routinely comprised of many attributes, properties, relationships and so forth but something indispensable is present within every one of them and nothing else is as significant about human beings as this element about them. No doubt, their capacity for friendship and family, not to mention corporate and team efforts, is immense and vital to their lives. Still, what is most significant about them is who they are, not their membership in families, groups, nations. In other words, to be human is to be first and foremost an individual because of the capacity of each to create a life, to forge his or her character and the resulting kind of life that is his or hers alone. Human beings do not belong to other, more important beings, whatever communitarians and other collectivists would maintain.

Individualism had been caricatured, and occasionally defended, in an atomistic version. Atomistic or radical individualism, derived from Thomas Hobbes, sees human beings as unique, with no real human—and thus social—nature at all. This has led to a subjectivist ethics and even politics, whereby the only principles of conduct that are binding upon us all are those we have chosen to accept.[2]

In contrast, Rand's individualism may be characterized as classical or humanistic. The nature of human individuality is identified in terms consistent with the idea that everything has a nature—a justified fitting classification. In the case of human beings this nature gives rise to the potential of a very substantial dimension of individuality—self-directedness, self-governance, personal responsibility, creativity, originality, novelty—in the life of every person.

Why was Rand such a fervent, insistent individualist and how does her project fare? Rand answers the first questions in an essay that addresses her own career, that she wanted to make it possible for herself to write about human beings as they ought to be, not as they usually are. The worldview she sought to express as an aspiring novelist, she points out, had been woefully absent from the culture.[3] What she found to be widely embraced is naturalism or some sort of absurdism. This required, Rand tells us, that she turn to the development of a philosophical system.

Rand explains that she realized that only if she first develops a rational, reality-based philosophy of human nature would there exist a foundation and context for her romantic realist fiction. Such an "ideal" would have to be complex and non-utopian, and inspire men and women to admire and defend the social and political system suitable for its realization, namely, capitalism.[4]

This work by Rand produced her literary artistry, via her plays and novels, and Objectivism, by way of her philosophical writings. These combined to provide a passionately expressed and thoughtfully sketched philosophical foundation for a rational moral and political system and an individualist vision of human life, arguably superior to all other systems that were live options in the intellectual atmosphere.

Rand did not advance a vision in the sense of some impossible ideal, a perfect but unattainable goal for which to aim in life. That is how visions are often understood, as "impossible dreams," "utopias." Ayn Rand develops a moral vision that by her own account she firmly anchors in reality: it projects a conception of human life that accords with the highest yet realistic standards of human living.

Rand believes that happiness is the highest ethical goal for human beings to pursue.

> Happiness is that state of consciousness which proceeds from the achievement of one's values. If a man values productive work, his happiness is the measure of his success in the service of his life. But if a man values destruction, like a sadist—or self-torture, like a masochist—or life beyond the grave, like a mystic—or mindless 'kicks,' like the reckless driver of a hotrod car—*his* alleged happiness is the measures of his success in the service of his own destruction....[5]

By Rand's account, however, it isn't sufficient for a culture to give even the fullest expression, correct as it may be, to the political framework that makes such happiness possible. It is necessary for there to be the widespread, prevalent conviction of the merits of the moral vision that places happiness at the pinnacle of human achievement. This vision, thus, needs to be widely embraced and continually promulgated by a community's intellectuals, artists, and others who trade in ideas.

Rand's American Individualism

Rand acknowledged that America gave substantially sound voice to the political principles that best accommodate human living in the pursuit of happiness. Consider how clearly the Declaration of Independence gives them expression:

> We hold these truths to be self-evident, that all men are created equal, that they are endowed by their Creator with certain unalienable Rights, that among these are Life, Liberty and the pursuit of Happiness. That to secure these rights, Governments are instituted among Men, deriving their just powers from the consent of the governed.

Despite the political sense and vision of the Declaration, its connection to a philosophical point of view needs to be spelled out for the citizenry. Without that they will remain convinced by the critics and detractors that it is merely a framework for the fulfillment of greedy motives. As Abraham Lincoln noted in 1859:

> All this [the economic success of America] is not the result of accident. It has a philosophical cause. Without the *Constitution* and the *Union*, we could not have attained the result; but even these are not the primary cause of our great prosperity. There is something back of these, entwining itself more closely about the human heart. That something, is the principle of 'Liberty

to all' — the principle that clears the *path* to all — gives *hope* to all — and, by consequence, *enterprise*, and *industry* to all.[6]

Contrary to the critics of the American polity — who still haven't stopped their refrain, even after their prized alternative of socialism has been repeatedly discredited — the priority of commerce or exchange is not implied in the American social system, even if we admit that it "clears the path to...enterprise, and industry to all." Common sense plainly shows this, even in the face of widespread accusations about the necessary economic motivations of all human action and thought.

The principle of liberty to all is not embraced within the American political tradition merely because this tradition rests on the view supposedly shared by Hobbes and Locke that "life is the joyless quest for joy."[7] Art, science, the press, religion, and other endeavors, all make ample use of this principle in the effort human beings exert to flourish, along with the efforts spent on economic advances.

Of course, without the philosophical underpinnings spelled out in support of individual liberty, the charge that greed motivates the embrace of the free system — often given support by professional economists — could be made palatable. That explains why even as serious an admirer of Rand as ABC-TV news correspondent John Stossell titled his one-hour special discussion of capitalism "Greed," not, for instance, "Enterprise" or even "Trade"![8] So, in light of the mistaken association of the free society with mere economic considerations about human life, Rand attempted to identify clearly and systematically the ethical principles that gave support to the American system of a free society, including its capitalist political economy. She argued, as we have already seen in earlier section of this work, that those ethical principles are sound — based on a well-developed philosophical and scientific understanding of human nature — and that in a somewhat imprecise way the Founders comprehended them. Since they were focused on politics, however, they did not make it their point to provide the ethical basis for the political system they thought made the best sense for human community living. So Rand set out to do the philosophical work she deemed necessary. As we saw, that philosophical work amounted to no small feat, especially if one considers that Rand aspired primarily to be a novelist, not a professional philosopher.

Capitalism as Implied by Individualism

Rand's point was that more is required than politics and a merely *implicit* ethics in order to give justice, as understood in the classical liberal tradition, a solid foundation. Without a firm philosophical base that is widely enough embraced throughout its culture, the free system *is* vulnerable to even some of the more feeble objections from critics, ones that can slowly weaken and in time destroy it. This is not some ideological point, either. It is not as if in order to sustain the life of a free system such as America came close to being, Rand manufactured some philosophical notions that made the system appear palatable. Despite many instances to the contrary, Rand is not an ideologue, one who rationalizes pre-set sentiments or desires with pseudo-arguments. Her motto, "check your premises," is a clarion call for honest philosophizing, whatever its ultimate result.

Some critics of American capitalism have made the valid point that this system of economic arrangements has yet to be widely and prominently associated with a comprehensive philosophical ethics. It thus lacks moral fuel.

Indeed, even more broadly put, the problem with Western liberal capitalism is that the political liberty it cherishes (at least in the language of its political declarations) has not been adequately justified by the pursuit of human excellence. As Solzhenitsyn noted: "A society without any objective legal scale is a terrible one indeed. But a society with no other scale but the legal one is not worthy of man either."[9] Others, such as the highly celebrated Russian born English philosopher Isaiah Berlin, have gone so far as to claim that the free system cannot have a moral foundation because of the plurality of ethical values in human life, ones that do not form any kind of hierarchy and which cannot be given some universal justification. Berlin approvingly attributes to Machiavelli the discovery that ends "equally ultimate, equally sacred, may contradict each other; [and] that entire systems of value may come into collision without possibility of rational arbitration, and not merely in exceptional circumstances, as a result of abnormality or accident or error . . . but as part of the normal human situation."[10] From this, namely that there are multiple *and* conflicting moral values that are equally valid guides for our lives, we can infer that no moral order exists to support the political system that best accommodates this very fact about human living.[11]

Rand's ethical theory of rational egoism or individualism aims, in contrast, to be both objectively valid and sufficiently multi-faceted so as to meet both of the challenges posed by the critics. For Rand, being rational—i. e., acting rationally, thoughtfully, by the guidance of the results of sharp conceptual focus of one's mind—is the prime moral virtue for everyone. So, since rationality can take full account of differences among people—rational decisions will guide one to practical actions that have been forged in light of the particulars of a person's situation, taking all relevant facts into consideration—there will be no demand for universal values suited only for special groups or particular persons.[12]

In consequences, as far as politics or law is concerned, it is possible to demonstrate that critics are wrong to claim that the American capitalist system lacks moral support or, more harshly, is crass, callous, heartless, nihilistic, purely legalistic, and incapable of inspired support and defense. Instead, as noted already, capitalism—the social system that has at its political foundation the principles announced in the Declaration of Independence—contains certain broad and widely applicable normative elements that focus on the necessary aspects of human social life. Even if understood solely as an economic system, capitalism is amply attentive to values by fostering the conditions for personal responsibility via its exclusion of force from human relationships. The individual's initiative is the prime requirement for the achievement of prosperity, whatever the ingredients of that might be, with the clear requirement that others' efforts must not be obstructed and thus need to be legally respected. This carries ample moral substance. Thus, contrary to the critics' charge, Rand stresses that economics is itself a discipline that rests on certain moral notions—property rights, prudence, the value of providing for one's and one's loved ones' needs and wants, which is to say, for prosperity.

The problem Rand addressed is that, while the political principles of capitalism in the main require every individual to lead the moral life, those political principles are neither sufficient as a moral code nor firmly linked philosophically to such a code. And no well-developed solution to this problem has been in place in Western cultures. Instead, two attitudes toward the problem have dominated the works of moral theoreticians—philosophers, theologians, and pedagogues.[13]

The first attitude, exhibited in our day by the theologians Michael Novak and Robert Sirico, sees a need for religious ethical traditions to be summoned to the defense of capitalism. Loyalty and faith in something superior to human life are supposed to sustain the free society. The second attitude, which as we saw Berlin propounded, denies moral foundation for any sort of political system and then counsels muddling through without given the system moral backing or, accordingly to many economists, on human drives, vested interests, and psychological or social instincts.

Normative Capitalism

Looking first at the last alternative, we can see that free society has come to be widely linked with its supposedly amoralist tenets. This is due in part to the mistaken association of modern economics with scientific neutrality (especially regarding moral or political values). The point may be stated as follows: modern economics is both scientific and gives support to the free market; introducing moral issues just weakens the scientific integrity of the case for liberty.

Those who have sought religious support for politics have, in turn, been willing to make compromises between liberty and slavery. They have denied Lincoln's premise that "no man is good enough to govern another man, *without that other's consent*"[14] mainly on grounds of faith and tradition. For these individuals (mainly America's conservatives), liberty is a fine and productive thing, but in the end, various moral requirements call for its denial as a general principle of human relationships. Those taking this line find the very idea of rational morality socially destructive, since that would place human beings in a position of self-reliance—reliance upon their own reason.

The welfare-state alternative is but the secular version of the faith that there must be something outside the individual human being and his personal excellence to which each of us owes allegiance. Attempts to ground this supposed allegiance on a sound philosophy have ended in appeals to intuition, utopian visions, and theories of historical progress toward a glorious future all of us are obligated to usher in. None of these efforts are satisfactory for purposes of grounding a political system, because in none of these is it possible to establish the case for the system objectively so that everyone with normal conceptual and perceptual faculties might arrive at the same conclusions concerning the kind of system best suited for human beings.

Both economic and spiritual welfare statists have rejected any defense of capitalism based on a moral footing. Those who do try to defend capitalism have rejected the possibility of a rational normative approach. But, in fact, capitalist society cannot be given sound support unless the rights of *all* individuals can be shown to be founded on sound, rational, objectively established moral theory. This demonstrates that while altruistic considerations have their place in human relations, they do not play a decisive role or justify depriving others of liberty.

Morality for Human Living

Adam Smith observed that modern moral philosophy is defective, and the defect to which he pointed suggests that a better philosophical approach to morality would be supportive of the free society:

> Ancient moral philosophy proposed to investigate wherein consisted the happiness and perfection of a man, considered not only as an individual, but as the member of a family, or a state, and of the great society of mankind. In that philosophy, the duties of human life were treated of as subservient to the happiness and perfection of human life. But, when moral as well as natural philosophy came to be taught only as subservient to theology, the duties of human life were treated of as chiefly subservient to the happiness of a life to come. In the ancient philosophy, the perfection of virtue was represented as necessarily productive to the person who possessed it, of the most perfect happiness in this life. In the modern philosophy, it was frequently represented as almost always inconsistent with any degree of happiness in this life, and heaven was to be earned by penance and mortification, not by the liberal, generous, and spirited conduct of a man. By far the most important of all the different branches of philosophy became in this manner by far the most corrupted.[15]

At this juncture, Rand's work has to be considered, for it is this ancient perspective on the moral life of human beings that she has resurrected — without the flaws contained in its renditions in ancient thought — (e.g., its metaphysical idealism and its reification of abstract, collective humanity).

What Rand shows is that man has an objective need for morality, and that the morality appropriate to satisfy this need is one in which "the duties of human life [are] subservient to the happiness and perfection of human life."[16] The ethical theory of rational self-interest, articulated throughout Rand's philosophical works and displayed in her fiction, returns to a view advanced by Aristotle, among others, as to the place and function of morality in human life. But when applied within the sphere of human community life, Rand's ethics of rational self-interest implies a political system of capitalism in its purest form, not the semi-paternalistic ideal of Aristotle's polity.

Also, Rand's idea of rational self-interest is different from the Hobbesian and neo-Hobbesian versions of egoism. The reason both Randian ethics and Hobbesian ethics are referred to as egoistic or individualistic is that in each, the individual is placed at the pinnacle of the hierarchy of values in human existence, and in neither is any alternative arrangement seen. But, the self for Rand is different from what it is for, and the principles of morality that flow from these two forms of egoism are clearly different.

Anti-Idealism?

The most important criticism of Rand's ethical teaching in our context is hinted at by Michael Novak, who states that to ask humans to seek their own flourishing in life is insufficient inspiration and is, thus, socially and politically self-destructive. To guarantee the self-perpetuation of the social system, we need a moral vision. To place the individual at the highest point of our value scale simply is not inspiring enough.[17] It is true that an individualist or egoist cannot construct a collective moral vision. Rand's ethical theory, however, enables each of us to construct our own personal — but always human — ideal; and her philosophical inquiry demonstrates that that is everything there can and should be to a moral vision.

Another more complex objection to the individualist foundation of capitalism is advanced by Leo Strauss. In his characterization of Locke's view of human nature, Strauss remarks that "Through the shift of emphasis from natural duties or obligations to natural rights, the individual, the ego, had become the center and origin of the moral world, since man — as distinguished from man's end — had become the center or origin."[18] Strauss sees the base of morality in the liberal ethos, not as an ideal to be reached, but as a need to be satisfied. For Strauss, the individual denies the idea of a *summum bonum* — some highest good toward which to aspire — and "in the absence of *summum bonum*, man would lack completely a star and compass for his life if there were no *summum malum*"[19] — a worst evil from which to escape (e.g., the death of oneself). However, Rand's view is that man is an end in himself qua man, i.e., that the realization of the rational capacity in one's particular life is a *summum bonum*. She thereby rejects the possibility of separating human life and human good.[20]

From analyses such as Strauss's, many have concluded that liberal capitalism, the free society, cannot be morally justified. If it is true that only by reference to the idea that human beings are driven (by genes, history, evolutionary forces, or instinct) can the free society be defended, the foregoing conclusions follow. But the conclusion is ill founded: it is possible, clearly, that the type of society defended on neo-Hobbesian grounds can also be defended on a different understanding of human existence. It may be true that if the Hobbesian viewpoint is correct, then capitalism suits us well. But, it is false that if the Hobbesian view is wrong, then capitalism does not suit us well.

Ultimately, the capacity of a moral theory to provide a bona fide moral vision (as opposed to a fraudulent, utopian vision) confirms the truth of that theory. A valid moral vision is a functional ideal, not an impossible dream. It will inspire good human beings to defend the conditions that make this ideal possible. But, if what Novak and other newfound supporters of capitalism are asking for is a magic formula that can generate an inspired defense of society, then nothing will satisfy them.

Humans may not always be guided by truth, but when they are guided by falsehood, the likelihood of frustration is so great that cynicism will result. What has prevented cynicism wherever corrupt moralities have taken root is an ad-mixture of common sense. Thus, the self-sacrifice that is part of most moralities is tempered with a requirement for honesty and integrity — virtues that promote anything but one's demise. But, it is undeniable that cynicism has closed in frequently enough in human history. If it is true today that the West has lost its will, it is true because we lack a sound moral code that nurtures realistic and robust moral visions.

The Purpose of a Moral Vision

In what sense does Rand's work enable one to create a moral vision? For Rand, as for Aristotle, the question "How should a human community be organized?" can only be answered after the question "How should I, a human being, live my life?" has been answered. Rand follows the Greek tradition of regarding politics as a sub-field of ethics, although she envisions the actual substance of these two fields in ways distinct enough to make it necessary to consider her views on their own. For Rand, the right way to live is the ground on which to establish the basic principles governing interpersonal behavior. These principles of community conduct establish the appropriate principles that govern political life.[21]

A moral vision is an image of the state of affairs that arises from living by a particular code of ethics. Virtually any moral point of view offers something akin to a moral vision for those who care to formulate it. Theologically based ethics have been accompanied by an otherworldly vision—a state of ultimate bliss—that would result from leading the moral life on earth. In secular altruistic moralities, images of the (loving) brotherhood of all men (such as that promised in the communist future) are envisioned. The function of such images is to remind one of the concrete implications of subscribing to the life of virtue. In practical terms, the images encourage loyalty to the principles being promoted.

A central feature of the persistent criticism of liberal, democratic capitalism has been that it fails to project an inspiring moral vision. Within the tradition of capitalism, the value of liberty is socially paramount. However, liberty is by definition an absence of coercion, an absence of an evil. Liberty is not the presence of a concrete achievement; although, when possessed of liberty, a free individual can create a concrete good.

So, liberalism admittedly lacks a complete moral vision, since it has been focused mainly on politics and economics. One of liberalism's greatest virtues, namely its relegation of politics to a discrete realm of human life, is turned against it by a wide variety of collectivist demands. Indeed, it is a contradiction to demand that liberalism offers, in the context of a theory of limited politics, a total moral vision. Yet, what liberalism has achieved is to conceive of a political order in conformity with human nature—a system which requires that each individual carry full responsibility for one's own moral achievements and failures. Only where others would obstruct this individual responsibility may the government—the instrument of man's political concerns—make a move, not for any other purpose. Is this liberalism's emergence?

Irving Kristol puts it this way: "The enemy of liberal capitalism is not so much socialism as nihilism."[22] If by this, Kristol means that liberal capitalism can amount to a sound political system only if its political features alone can avoid nihilism—the abnegation of values—then he accepts the collectivist assumption that it is the function of politics to supply the full substance of morality. This assumption is in direct conflict with the individualist foundations of the capitalist system; and if these ethical foundations are sound, Kristol is simply asking for the impossible.

Rand's Moral-Political Vision

Rand enables us to construct for ourselves a moral vision that is not so deceptively simple as the theocratic and collectivist alternatives. The payoff is that each individual can achieve a credible, realizable moral vision that incorporates private and public (i.e., distinctively political) components. Such a vision is not simple, because it takes into account the individuality of everyone, as well as everyone's essential humanity. Since individuality thus conceived does not occupy some inferior metaphysical and moral position—as with Plato and Marx—it has to be regarded seriously. However, individualism does not boil down to mere quantitative significance, as it does within a nominalist/atomist framework. The idea of the individual as it emerged from the atomistic tradition could not withstand attacks such as Marx's against liberalism, since, as the latter observed, "the freedom in question is that of a man treated as an isolated monad and withdrawn into himself."[23]

In Rand's metaphysics, the particular and universal are inseparable. Accordingly, her principles of moral conduct support a moral vision of both aspects of each individual's life—humanity and individuality—equally and inseparably. Each person's excellence involves the process of achieving and sustaining the human life that is one's own, requiring that there be upheld both a unity of person and a separateness of each person from the other.

From an individualist perspective, basic virtues would still guide the life of a good person. But, the results of the implementation of these virtues cannot be assimilated into a uniformly applicable concrete picture. Each person can have a moral vision, but there can be no collective moral vision. In lieu of a collectivist vision, Rand establishes a vision of the moral life as it applies to basic human relationships in a political context from the very beginning of her writing. *Anthem*, her novella, stresses the voluntariness of all adult human relations as the mark of full civilization. *The Fountainhead* develops why that should be so as a matter of the proper ethics for human life, while *Atlas Shrugged* sketches the entire philosophical framework that backs up those ideas.

The political vision she champions makes considerable demands upon us, for it must be filled in by each of us with concrete content. It postulates the individual's aspiration to excellence, but precludes any guarantee that this social moral vision will be achieved. To give this personal moral vision of individualism public expression is a difficult artistic task indeed. Certain forms of art serve as the medium for this purpose. The novel, play, ballet, and painting all are media for such expression of more or less widely applicable moral visions that exalt and inspire. Unfortunately, this domain of feeling associated with the arts has been almost the exclusive province of religion. Rand explains:

> Religion's monopoly in the field of ethics has made it extremely difficult to communicate the emotional meaning and connotation of a rational view of life. Just as religion has preempted the field of ethics, turning morality against man, so it has usurped the highest moral concepts of our language, placing them outside this earth and beyond man's reach.[24]

Given the long history of religion's dominance in the arts and the somewhat belated full tolerance of secular artistic expression, it is to Rand's artistic credit that, despite her unambiguous atheism, some have proclaimed her a profoundly religious writer. The meaning of E. Merrill Root's praise of her, for example, is none other than that she has been able to inspire and produce exaltation with her artistry and that many people have no way of explaining this other than by linking it with something mystical, despite the rational philosophical foundations of all of Rand's ideas and imagery.

Nihilism versus Secular Morality

It is imperative that those who are concerned with the spiritual revitalization of the West stress the need for a rational morality and an individualist moral vision. But, will these be adequate to counter nihilism? Once again, consider Irving Kristol:

> In every society, the overwhelming majority of the people lead lives of considerable frustration, and if society is to endure, it needs to be able to rely on a goodly measure of stoical resignation. In theory, this could be philosophical rather than religious; in fact, philosophical stoicism has always been an aristocratic prerogative; it has never been able to give an acceptable rationale of "one's station and one's duties" to those whose stations are low and duties are onerous.[25]

With certain widely, though implicitly, accepted assumptions embedded in these observations, what Kristol is saying seems almost commonplace. Hardly anyone is always satisfied, and we all know of some who are entirely desperate, even in the best of times. Does it follow that, for such people to have hope, something of a fancy story—a Platonic "noble lie"—must sustain them?

Not so, once the assumptions are made explicit. First, Kristol flatly accepts the view that at root, morality consists of duties. So conceived, a morally excellent life comes down to a life dominated by chores. This makes it plausible that, to live a moral life, one would need some inducement or incentive beyond life itself—in Adam Smith's terms, "to be earned only by penance and mortification, by the austerities and abasement of a monk."

Second, in Kristol's detached framework, the issue of the truth of religion seems to be set entirely aside. From his god's-eye point of view, religion has, in fact, no basis; yet he, unlike the rest of us, is in possession of the aristocratic prerogative and sees that we need religion. If "in theory" morality could be defended philosophically, then religion is not indispensable unless human beings are somehow naturally divided into those who can live with truth and those who require deception. That Kristol finds this the proper attitude toward his fellow humans is indicative of why he believes that life for most must be accepted stoically.

Despite the evidence that supports some of what Kristol says, we would be fooled by what is blatantly apparent—via newspapers, television, magazines, and the rhetoric of politics — to think that human life is as dismal as he reports. He fails to mention, for example, the private lives of millions who totally escape public notice, news reporting, and sociological inquiry. I am here focusing mostly on the quality of life linked to a so-called bourgeois society. In contrast, one need only examine reports from totalitarian states and consider the fate of millions who have lived through the epochs of feudalism, caesarism, and the varieties of Asian, Middle-Eastern, and African theocracies and tribal ages. Considering what we are these days said to have a natural right to (explained for example, in the United Nations Universal Declaration of Human Rights adopted in December 1948 and held up as a model of the just social system ever since), it is not difficult to see that despite appearances to the contrary, stoicism is not what is required. Granted that the state has rigged circumstances even in America so that the lives of many people are legally stymied (or kept artificially at a point of parasitic prosperity), it is only statistically true that these people lead lives of considerable deprivation and genuine frustration. This may be so at some point of some lives in some portions of the country, but in most cases there is no reason why this needs to remain so for each person individually.

There is, then, no reason to accept the pessimism Kristol projects. Neo-conservatives like him are correct to be concerned with morality, but they are misled about the nature of morality and what is required to explain it and give it force within our culture. They are thus playing into the hands of Marxists, whom they do not like, by seriously advocating religion as the opiate of the masses.

Do We Need Supernaturalism?

Throughout history in most countries, religion, with virtually absolute links to the state, has monopolized reflection — theorizing, teaching, and criticizing — about morality. Even in the United States, public education evolved very early, usually as a secular substitute for reliance on religious schooling. In both theocratic and democratic traditions, morality has retained its altruistic emphasis (as officially taught), in the first instance stressing the primacy of one's duty to God, in the second one's duty to the state or one's fellows. (It bears noting, though, that this altruism is a phony — once one appreciates the promise of eternal bliss, it is nothing to devote one's life on earth, a mere 70 or so years, to service to others.) Since the message in both instances bodes ill for all those who are being addressed, it is not surprising that either a heaven or a role in making a future heaven-on-earth has been promised to achieve compliance.

Aside from other problems, the idea that hope lies in the revitalization of a supernaturalist religious moral perspective is a will-o'-the-wisp. All that is left is the secular version, which is why Marxism — the most extreme secular altruistic/collectivist perspective on human life — has fared so well in the absence of alternative normative positions. In the end, we need to keep in mind that pessimism about the capacity of a philosophical, secular ethics rests mainly on the prior acceptance of the view that ethics requires self-denial. This realization reaffirms the enormous influence of the modern outlook on ethics referred to by Adam Smith as requiring that "heaven [is] to be earned by penance and mortification, not by the liberal, generous, and spirited conduct of man."

But abandoning the pessimistic stance may be justified in the light of Rand's work, the paramount significance of which is that, from an ethical viewpoint, it makes the rational conceptualization of one's own happiness possible and its depiction in works of art a reality. Rand's ethics isn't the promise of making mankind perfect, but it is the promise of the possibility of self-perfection, of being the best person one can be in the context of one's existence. This requires, however, that humans undertake the supreme moral effort to think conscientiously and to live by the judgment of such conscientious thought — and nothing else.

Individualism versus Marxism

Among the numerous concerns that have stood in the way of accepting the possibility of a moral vision of rational egoism — individualism within the moral/political framework of capitalism — a final one demands rebuttal. We will explore more fully in the next chapter, but the main criticism here comes from Marxism in the lament that in social terms the ethics of self-interest means mere "egoistic calculation."

Does ethical egoism really resolve personal worth into exchange value? Is commerce satanic? Will human community life turn into a cash nexus if the ethics of egoism is applied in practice?

Rand may initially appear to be classified among those who reduce human relationships to exchange value. In John Galt's famous speech we are told, for example, that "We, who live by values, not by loot, are traders, both in matter and in spirit. A trader is a man who earns what he gets and does not give or take the unearned."[26]

A close look should make clear that this conception of trade has nothing to do with the *homo economicus* conceptions of human relationships. There is nothing purely materialistic in the trader image of man in Rand's viewpoint. For Rand, emphasis is on the *terms* of human relationships, not on their motivation or the alleged economic impetus for all human conduct. A rational egoist is not a utility maximizer, a calculating hedonist, but an individual who acts on principle, by reference to a code of values that is not reducible to, but merely subsumes (within a certain social domain), market values.

Rand anticipates the attempt to dismiss her position by those who assimilate it within the materialist, reductionist tradition. She distinguishes between the sort of subjective value (or revealed preference) stressed by economists and some other defenders of the free society as the only meaningful value and the value various anti-capitalist critics find to be in need of emphasis. Rand notes that "the market value of a product does not reflect its philosophically objective value, but only its socially objective value.... [The former is] estimated from the standpoint of the best possible for man, i.e., by the criterion of the most rational mind possessing the greatest knowledge, in a given category, in a given period, and in a defined context." The latter is "the sum of the individual judgments of all the men involved in trade at a given time, the sum of what *they* valued, each in the context of his own life."[27]

So, unlike the economic advocates of the free market, Rand does not equate all types of values—artistic, economic, moral, and scientific. In the marketplace where people know very little of each other, exchange value may indeed be as close a measure of personal worth (between those involved in trade) as can reasonably be expected of the traders. A good chef will gain esteem as such; a bad taxi driver will fail to do so. It is probable that outside of economic engagements, individuals reach levels of nobility or dishonor not evident in the marketplace, yet there is no lament about the indifference shown such values in commercial relationships. One does not require the total recognition of one's worth or worthlessness from others one knows but slightly.

The market does not prevent a rational communication of value between those who trade with each other, but it does not fancy itself the court of last resort in these matters, contrary to what collectivists imagine to be required for human self-esteem. As Nathaniel Branden explains:

> Under capitalism, men are free to *choose* their 'social bonds' — meaning, to choose whom they will associate with. Men are not trapped within the prison of their family, tribe, caste, class, or neighborhood. They choose whom they will value, whom they will befriend, whom they will deal with, what kind of relationships they will enter. This implies and entails man's responsibility to form independent judgments. It implies and entails, also, that a man must earn the social relationships he desires.[28]

Replying to Erich Fromm, one of capitalism's long-time severest neo-Marxist critics, Branden shows just how misconceived is the view that "the principle underlying capitalist society and the principle of love are incompatible."[29] Fromm, following the early Marx (who followed Ludwig Feuerbach), advocates in effect that the intimacy of love between persons can be grafted onto the human race at large. Capitalism is unacceptable, since it does not adjust itself to this fantasy and instead makes "the fairness ethic ... the particular ethical contribution of capitalist society."[30]

But Fromm's idea and corresponding program are an illusion and horror chamber, as recent history has shown so vividly. Contrary to what some stubborn apologists for Marx still cling to — namely, the view that the Marxist-inspired (though not *caused*) Soviet Union, Stalinism, gulags, and other totalitarian evils throughout the world are merely perversions of an essentially human philosophy — Marxism, as Leszek Kolakowsky has observed, may not have been "predestined to become the ideology of the self-glorifying Russian Bureaucracy ... [but] it contained essential features, as opposed to accidental and secondary ones, that made it adaptable for this purpose."[31] To try to make mankind conform to an ideal suited to how one or two people might, if very good and very lucky, relate to each other in personal intimacies is to bring forth barbarism and inner death.

Subsuming some human relationships within the economic exchange framework is not only inoffensive, but morally commendable, even inspiring. Trading with the grocery clerk or plumber, we can only feign close friendship, unless we come to know each other very well by spending a great deal of time together. Close relations require knowledge and appreciation of a person's history, aspirations, character, dreams, foibles, tastes, and so forth. Unless we come to know a person as an individual, we deal with him more justly by rewarding him for the little he has in fact done for us in engaging in a particular transaction. We each can leave the market and find ourselves being appreciated by others for different reasons, and we always have as a last and maybe best resort our own self-esteem. To fantasize about a closer relationship is to build utopian dreams that are the stuff of fairy tales, not of political philosophy.

What we can and should do is pay persons the respect due them for having done admirable work. Via the money we exchange, provided it represents value (honest earnings, not officially inflated "notes"), both can assume the work as well enough done so others might enter the same transaction. In a free market, it is this basic trust we can ask of our relations with one another. We can even begin to become friends. All over the world, every hour of the day, humans befriend each other. But it is false that they are duty-bound to do so and intolerable that they should be forcibly organized accordingly.

Justice and Market Exchanges

One lamented consequence of our market dealings — as of some non-market ones — is the possibility of benefiting persons of whom, if one knew them, one would disapprove. One might, indeed, be exchanging value with a serious enemy: A Jew might inadvertently trade with an anti-Semite, neither knowing that the other is an antagonist.

Yet, is there really something drastically wrong with this? After all, in a free marketplace, boycotts and economic pressures of all types are possible, unlike in socialist and other planned economies. In general, the beneficial consequences of market impartiality — the concrete result of the "fairness ethic" — are considerable. Most of this is evident from common sense and is obscured only when we view the world with ideological blinders.

Those who dream of a society that will guarantee for everyone a collective utopian vision will always find the free society objectionable. Those who discuss the moral foundations of capitalism and its capacity to sustain a moral vision are usually theoreticians who assess the issues with the aid of elaborate theories. Or they are unaware of the theoretical support for laissez-faire capitalism, so they tend to accept the distorted history, handed down under ideological influences, that is hostile to capitalism.

Commerce can appear to be satanic to such individuals, especially if they have accepted impossible ideals by which to evaluate political systems and have not questioned the belief that capitalist societies are to be on the model of a boxing ring. In the tradition of Aristotelian[32] (not Hobbesian) ethical theories, personal economic well-being is one aspect of a larger concern for all human life. Thus, capitalist human relations need not be crass.

Rand's ethical conception of human life, personal and social, enables one to sustain a moral vision that is both realistic and exalting—capable of inspiring humans to heights never before attempted. To date, however, Rand has not received her due from the intellectual community as an advocate of the philosophical and ethical base of free society. Although her novels have been bestsellers since their original publication, intellectuals have merely alluded to her ideas in asides. Rand's observation on this topic is instructive: "It is only the American people—not the intellectuals—who have given signs of rebellion against altruism. It is a blind, groping, ideologically helpless rebellion. But it would be a terrible crime of history if that rebellion is allowed to be defeated by silent default."[33]

Unfortunately, such default appears to be in the making today. Those intellectuals who would speak of the need for spiritual fuel must recognize the supreme social importance of liberty; and those who value liberty must value morality, the fuel of the spirit. The likes of Peter Unger and Peter Singer, for example, who are repeatedly advocating altruism, the placing of others, even of animals, ahead of the individual human being's rational self-interest, are a testimony to the logic of Rand's concern.

Yet, matters can change, and to any who would seriously consider a change for the better, Rand's words could be of considerable value: "Now is the time to assert, to proclaim and to uphold the ideas that created America—and thus save this country and, incidentally, to offer guidance to a perishing world. But, this cannot be done without rejecting the morality of altruism."[34] While this may appear hyperbolic to many, it is, if what Rand has worked for has any merit at all, a serious warning.

The human species, Rand teaches, is best guided by an ethical system in terms of which every individual ought to place his or her own human flourishing or success as a rational animal — including a social and political being — in first place on one's list of priorities. That is what Randian — what I have called "classical" — individualism proposes and it is most likely the ethics that is conducive to human living.

In Rand's social political philosophy, the point of politics, as it relates to human social life, is the objective need human beings have for the just adjudication of disputes. Just adjudication is obtainable by way of the establishment of a system of objective laws, ones that rest on human nature, namely, basic individual rights. Once such a system is in place, the due process that will ensue if proper vigilance is exerted by administrators of justice, legal decisions will emerge that best express in the myriad of particular instances what amount to just decisions.

Such a vision of political order may not suit idealist utopians who would wish politics to address all the problems we face in our lives. But it will indeed amount to a proper moral vision as far as our organized social life is concerned.

Endnotes

1   The next person to mention in this connection is David L. Norton, whose book *Personal Destinies, A Philosophy of Ethical Individualism* (Princeton, NJ: Princeton University Press, 1976), is a revolutionary break with the Kantian flavor of most of contemporary moral philosophy.

2   For more on this, see Tibor R. Machan, *Classical Individualism* (London: Routledge, 1998).

3   Ayn Rand, "The Goal of My Writing." *Objectivist Newsletter*, October 1963, pp. 37-42.

4   Rand insisted on calling her politics "capitalist," just as she insisted in calling her ethics "egoist," in part as a kind of "in your face" protest against those who would yield to popular sentiments and, by her light, misunderstandings regarding these terms. "Selfishness" is usually taken to mean something heartless and even injurious toward others but Rand thought this meaning is predicated on a misguided view of human nature, of the self. Similarly, she didn't wish to cave in to the Marxist pejorative idea of capitalism as a system of exploitation (of workers by capitalists). She even rejected the label "libertarian" because she believed

too many who are so called fail to support the system by way of a rational philosophy.

5   Op cit., *The Virtue of Selfishness*, p. 28.

6   Quoted in Harry V. Jaffa, *How to Think about the American Revolution* (Durham, NC: Carolina Academic Press, 1978, p. 1.

7   That Hobbes and Locke share this view is alleged by Leo Strauss, *Natural Right and History*, 2d ed. (Chicago: University of Chicago Press, 1970), p. 251. I address this issue further in Tibor Machan, "Libertarianism and Conservatives," *Modern Age* 24 (Winter, 1980). But see John P. East, "The American Conservative Movement of the 1980's" ibid., for a different view.

8   Of course, Stossell and ABC-TV may well have chosen the term for its sensational connotation, given the importance of attractive viewers to his TV program.

9   Alexander Solzhenitsyn, "A World Slit Apart," *Imprimis* 7 (1978): 4.

10   Isaiah Berlin, "The Originality of Machiavelli," in Berlin, *Against the Current*, ed. H. Hardy (New York: Penguin Books: 1982), especially pp. 74-75.

11   Not that Berlin himself didn't prefer the liberal polity to others. It appears, however, he did not think any moral case could be made for it.

12   There is a thorough discussion of this point in Douglas J. Den Uyl, "Teleology and Agent-Centeredness." *The Monist*, vol. 75 (January 1992).

13   There are other approaches to take, but all are so hostile to liberty as not to bear discussion. There are extremes of the left and the right where liberty is not even regarded as a value—let alone the necessary social pre-condition for many other values to flourish—so the suggestion of a compromise between liberty and some version of slavery does not arise. (According to these views the individual is not even a whole entity or being but merely a part belonging to a real and important whole, such as humanity, the nation, race, family, tribe or ethnic group.) Various theocratic political doctrines on the right and totalitarian views on the left would fit this characterization.

14   Quoted in Jaffa, *American Revolution*, pp. 1-2.

15   Adam Smith, *The Wealth of Nations* (New York: Random House, 1937), p. 726.

16   Ayn Rand, "The Objectivist Ethics," op. cit., pp. 13-35.

17   Michael Novak, *The American Vision* (Washington, DC: American Enterprise Institute, 1978), seems to argue this point with the support of, e.g., Bernard-Henri Levi. More recently George Glider, in *Wealth and Poverty* (New York: Basic Books, 1980), which is regarded as a brilliant Christian, anti-rationalist defense of capitalism, stresses the view that only an ethics of altruism can defend the free market, by reference to the notion that as an act of faith, each person should seek to create, to engage in entrepreneurship and trade, with the motivation of helping others, not of furthering his own proper ends.

18   Strauss, *Natural Right and History*, p. 251.

19   Ibid.

20   Ayn Rand, *For the New Intellectual* and *The Virtue of Selfishness*.

21   Ayn Rand, *For the New Intellectual* (New York: New American Library, 1961), p. 182.

22   Irving Kristol, "Capitalism, Socialism, and Nihilism," *Public Interest* (Spring 1973), p. 8.

23   Karl Marx, *Selected Writings*, ed. David McLellan (New York: Oxford University Press, 1977), p. 53.

24   Ayn Rand, *The Fountainhead* (New York: New American Library, 1968, P. ix. See, in this connection, E. Merrill Root, "What about Ayn Rand?" *National Review*, January 30, 1960, pp. 76-78.

25   Kristol, "Capitalism, Socialism, and Nihilism," p. 12.

26   Ayn Rand, *Atlas Shrugged* (New York: Random House, 1957), p. 1022.

27   Ayn Rand, "What is Capitalism?" in *Capitalism: The Unknown Ideal* (New York: New American Library, 1967), pp. 24-25.

28   Nathaniel Branden, "Alienation," *Objectivist Newsletter* 4 (1965): 37.

29   Quoted ibid., p. 36.

30   Quoted ibid.

31   Quoted in Michael Harrington, review of *Main Currents of Marxism*, by Leszek Kolakowski, *New Republic*, February 2, 1979, p. 32.

32   See W. F. Hardie, "The Final Good in Aristotle's Ethics," *Philosophy* 40 (1965): 277-95, for a discussion of the egoistic aspects of Aristotle's ethics. But this should not be taken as a claim that Rand's case for egoism is the same as Aristotle's. See Tibor R. Machan, "Recent Work in Ethical Egoism," *American Philosophical Quarterly* 16 (1979): 1-15, for a discussion of various recent versions of egoism, Rand's included.

One interesting claim made with reference to Ayn Rand's version of ethical egoism is that she may have built into the nature of the human ego an element of sociality that renders the theory intuitively acceptable but at the expense of leaving nothing in it that is distinctively egoistic, focused primarily on one's own benefit as the overriding purpose of human conduct.

Actually, Rand's egoism may indeed be utterly unusual. In her view the very nature of ethics—when it exists at all—receives an answer that makes ethics egoistic from the start. Why should we worry about how to act? Because there is no innate drive that guides us to live in line with our nature, to live as it is fit for us to live. But then what does this fitness come to? Well, the flourishing or success of the individual human being qua human being. And if to be a human being does involve conduct that is concerned with the well-being of others—generosity, kindness, and so forth.—then so does the proper self-enhancing ethics of every person. See, Tibor R. Machan, *Classical Individualism* (Routledge, 1998), for additional discussion of this point.

33   Ayn Rand, *The Moral Factor* (Palo Alto: Palo Alto Book Service, 1976), p. 12.

34   Ibid.

Chapter 5:
Rand versus Marx

Not Infatuated with Communism

In Ayn Rand's works, there is a clear-cut antipathy toward communism. Unlike many intellectuals in the West, Rand never considered Marx's vision in the slightest degree. Rand wrote several novels and philosophical and political essays throughout her life outside the walls of academe, only recently gaining some recognition from within those walls. She was, most importantly, an unabashed champion of individualist capitalism, indeed, the only modern defender of that system of political economy on explicitly moral grounds. One may even safely suggest that Rand's project is best construed as establishing a rapprochement between the ancient and the modern philosophical worldviews, that is, showing that the modern achievements in science do not defeat the Greek conception of human nature involving a telos or specific objective, namely, to live rationally.[1]

Before anything else we should identify what few matters unite Rand and Marx. Both were friends of science and technology. Both also saw productive work as an essential element of the life of a human being. But Rand saw this fact from the viewpoint of someone who rejected metaphysical materialism and identified the faculty of reason as having the central role in guiding human conduct, while Marx believed that productivity is prompted by the environment in which we live—specifically the tools of production, which shape consciousness. So Rand saw the Marxian version as turning the truth on its head, ascribing achievement not to persons, in the last analysis, but to impersonal forces in nature.[2]

Marxism's Essential Anti-Individualism

The most important element of Marxism to remember for purposes of understanding Rand's anti-communism is Marx's claim that

"The human essence is the true collectivity of man."[3] Even earlier than this remark from the 1844 Manuscripts is Marx's frank exclamation, in his high school departure essay, that the greatest moral merit should befall those who devote themselves to humanity, not to any artistic, scientific, or similar specialized achievement: "When we have chosen the vocation in which we can contribute most to humanity, burdens cannot bend us because they are sacrifices for all. Then we experience no meager, limited egoistic joy, but our happiness belongs to millions, our deeds live on quietly but eternally effective, and glowing tears of noble men will fall on our ashes."[4]

Marxian humanism is through and through collectivist. Human beings for Marx are not just essentially, as Aristotle claims, but exclusively social—they are species beings. Their very identity is being part of the larger "organic whole" of humanity.[5] While, no doubt Marx hoped for and predicted the ultimate emancipation of the human individual,[6] the new human being for Marx was to be a collective being, one who lived through and for humanity, not for his own welfare or excellence.

Rand was thoroughly opposed to this Marxism. It was to Marxism as an implicit and repugnant value theory and morality that Rand's Objectivism may be compared with profit. There might be other candidates—for example, Marx's economic determinism and scientism; his historicism and amoralism; his socialism and communism. But these are not the most basic aspects of Marxism with which Rand found fault. Rand could appreciate someone who is intent upon solving problems, even if those problems did not get solved in the last analysis. What was unforgivable is Marx's deep-seated, reactionary, albeit often only implicit, altruism and collectivist politics. It is when the individual human being got short-shrifted that Rand found the theory beyond redemption.[7]

And clearly Marx demeaned the human individual when he projected that a good society would consist of members who have renounced their own happiness in favor of the collective welfare, their individuality in favor of their species being, their love of self for the love of humanity as a sort of concrete universal to the welfare of which individuals may be sacrificed.

Of course, it may be opposed to the above that Marx, as he understood human nature, was a champion of the human individual, rightly understood. He had hoped for the human individual's emancipation or development into a fully mature version of what he is now. The species being—or the political nature—of every person is what, ever since Aristotle pointed it out, had been thought to be part of human nature. In other words, one could claim that Marx simply modernized or rendered scientifically comprehensible the ancient Greek notion that man is a political, communal being.

But there are problems with this suggestion. For Marx, the "scientific" socialist, the development of the social-political nature of the human species is a historical process and ultimate necessity.[8] For Aristotle that development is in large measure an individual accomplishment.[9] The social nature of any person would have to be realized as a matter of right reason, choice, virtue. It is not something that will come about in time, as the development of fruit bearing comes about for a fruit tree or the development of old age comes about for each of us. Moreover, the social nature of a human being is to be realized for the sake of that human being, for his or her happiness in life, not for the sake of humanity at large.[10]

Because of the economic and historical determinism in Marx's philosophy, the role of individuality in human social and political life has to be seen as minimal.[11]

Marx's versus a Truncated Individualism

Marx contrasted his humanism with the atomistic individualism that he linked to the classical liberal tradition of political economy.[12] This neo-Hobbesian conception of the human individual was deterministic and embraced a purely subjective theory of values. In our own time, too, this is the most prominently advanced and focused upon defense of the kind of society that is the most welcoming host to capitalist economic arrangements: free trade, freedom of contract, competition; in short, laissez-faire economics.[13]

It is also notable that both the classical liberal supporters and the Marxist critics of capitalist society embraced, implicitly at least, utilitarianism. Adam Smith, for example, did not defend the free market system because it expressed the importance of the individual and his or her prospect for happiness. John Stuart Mill, although by no means oblivious to individual concerns, defended liberalism on grounds that it was the most effective way to advance the greatest happiness of the greatest number. Even Herbert Spencer argued for a kind of rational utilitarianism. And since the heyday of classical liberal ideas this basic element of the support for its tenets has not changed significantly. Ludwig von Mises advanced a subjective theory of value; F. A. Hayek was a sort of Humean utilitarian, who stressed how the free marketplace would best generate progress; Milton Friedman is essentially a neoclassical value subjectivist or skeptic who defends liberty because he prefers it and considers it most supportive of political freedom; and Robert Nozick, though in some respects a Kantian, argued for his version of libertarianism on grounds that a system of Lockean rights is most congruent with our moral intuitions that favor personal autonomy and with the pursuit of essentially subjective personal goals.[14]

Rand's Moral Opposition to Communism

None but Rand has ever defended the free market system on grounds that it is an essential feature of a just system of community life, one that is suitable to the achievement of the objectively understandable and specifiable happiness of the human individual. Most famous defenders of capitalism are economists and they complain mostly that socialism and communism just cannot work. Rand completely disagrees with Hayek, for example, who says that "[T]he desire for a collectivist system springs from high moral motives."[15] As she put it, "There is no hope at all so long as would-be defenders of individualism spout things like that!"[16] Instead, she provides a moral defense of the system with her out-and-out ethical egoism, not any kind of subjectivism, hedonism, or psychological egoism like those who usually argue for capitalism.[17] It is this insistence on her part that what counts for most in life is one's own happiness as a human individual—not some kind of general welfare or public interest or global human progress or service to others—that makes her a distinct and unique opponent of Marxism on grounds of what she argues is a bona fide humanistic ethics (unlike that of Marx's alleged humanism).

Of course, the most important issue is whether Rand's distinctive point of view has philosophical merit. Is it true?

One can assert all sorts of propositions against Karl Marx, Jesus Christ, or anyone else but fail to come up with sufficient support, not to mention a better alternative, to make it worth considering. Rand's radicalism—in that she is perhaps the only major author in the modern age who unabashedly defends a robust ethical egoism—would be just an oddity if it had little more going for it beside her fierce and passionately utilized linguistic powers. Her novels are eloquent and forceful affirmations of her form of individualism, no doubt. They have found a resonance with millions of readers and continue to do so even while others have fallen by the wayside.[18] But the crucial question is whether Rand has provided ideas that are sound. That, however, is for readers to ascertain for themselves.

Rand's Anti-Marxism

Let us note some aspects of the history of Rand's anti-Communism.[19]

As we have noted, in *We the Living* Rand speaks directly about the Soviet manifestation of communism. It is not deeply philosophical, although it touches on the crucial features of Marxian social, economic, and political thought.[20] Interestingly, one of the most appealing characters in the work begins as a committed, loyal communist whose virtue of honesty and sincerity Rand identifies in the novel and builds upon in her plot. Yet, the main character, Kira, is a fierce and natural individualist who speaks some of the early renditions of Rand's ethics and politics. It is remarkable that this book, published in 1936, gained Rand nothing but scorn and derision in the Western literary world.[21] Even to date no one within the prominent literary establishment has said how wrong it was to have paid Rand no attention when she was delineating, in fictional form, the horrors now commonly acknowledged about the former Soviet Union. It seems too much to ask to have some member of the cultural elite express regret about the lack of respect accorded Rand—at the time a budding novelist struggling with the English language—when nearly everyone at that echelon of society was beaming with enthusiasm about the New World.

It is worth recalling here, also, that on the literary front Rand was unique in this respect. If one contrasts her with the two major novelists who addressed the problems of totalitarian collectivist community life, namely, Aldous Huxley's *Brave New World* and George Orwell's *1984*, one notices a vital point of departure. Both Huxley and

Orwell at least implicitly credit such systems with the ability to develop and maintain a highly advanced form of technology and industrialization. Rand, however, does not. She denies that one can have both massive oppression of human individuality and the creativity needed for a prospering scientific society. Of course, the mere repetition of past technologies is not impossible in an oppressive society, yet even that would require some organization inventiveness, something that totalitarian societies would lack and fictional renditions of them ought to take note of.

This clear awareness of the connection between human individuality and creativity alone indicates Rand's depth of understanding of the flaws of totalitarian collectivism. It was without much doubt far greater than those of other literary figures who addressed the topic in their fictional works. Rand realized from the beginning that one of the main failings of such systems is that they squash human creativity, and thus human individual liberty.[22] Rand, in short, sees that slavery is bad in part because it undermines the will to innovate, to build, to advance. Her novella, *Anthem*, I have already noted, is a masterful literary testament to the link between individual liberty and a community life that enjoys the fruits of human creativity by showing that totalitarian collectivism is not only cruel, harsh, nasty, and brutish but, alas, bland, and boring.

It is fair, to recall that one of the major characteristics of Soviet society was its backwardness in simple technology, excepting only those parts of it which were stolen from the West or produced by the small class of extremely pampered scientists and artists. (Rand once noted that although she is a fierce anti-Communist, she didn't believe that the USSR needed to be feared militarily since a slave society cannot be expected to keep up a technology that would make its military competitive with societies that enjoyed substantial individual liberty.)

Yet Rand didn't indicate her understanding of the nature of human community life only by means of the action of her literary creations. She went on to produce a body of work that explicated her ideas and ideals about human life.

What, then, are the central differences between Rand and Marx? Why, furthermore, is the position Rand developed so potent in showing Marxism to be wrong?

To start with, Rand's metaphysics, as we have already seen, does not owe much to Hegel but to Aristotle. She embraces few ultimately fundamental laws—only the Law of Identity and the Law of Non-contradiction. These are implicit in the fundamental axiom she identified: existence exists, existence is identity, and consciousness is identification.

In contrast, Marx's metaphysics, to the extent that one may hold that he embraced at least some of what Engels said in this field, commits him to a substantive ontology of dialectical materialism. This is the best way to make sense of Marx's claim that history develops toward maturation—that the "organic body [or whole]"[23] that is, humankind must develop toward communism (which is not some ideal but a real future state, the way old age is for the development of a living entity). Although some claim this view is empirically based, that is highly doubtful—no one could observe evidence that is best organized to indicate such a historical materialism. It is the result of a certain kind of analysis based on the ontological status of the dialectic.

Secondly, Marx proposes an epistemology of reflectivism. (It was developed in some detail by Lenin. But the basics are there in Marx's works.) The human mind, as he argues, reflects reality. The phantoms that reach the brain implant in our consciousness a picture of reality. As a result what we believe is imprinted upon us and will vary depending on when this imprinting occurs and the circumstances to which we are exposed. Thus, by Marx's account, the consciousness of human beings is determined by their economic class membership, since it is that class membership that places them in certain material environments. Accordingly, members of classes generally must have the beliefs they have and no argument, only revolution, can alter their relationship to members of other classes. (This is where Marx's dialectics enters the realm of political economy—the clash of outlooks leads to unavoidable social upheavals that propel us to a new development of humanity.)

For Marx, thus, the individualist-capitalist way of understanding human social life reflects a given phase of historical development. It isn't that Locke, Smith, Ricardo, et al. were all wrong in what they thought in connection with economic and political life. They were mistaken to have generalized it, but then they could not really help themselves. Capitalism is true—for a given time in human history—but it will be overthrown, abolished, superseded, just as adolescence in an individual's biological-psychological life is superseded by young adulthood, which itself leads, necessarily, to maturity. By Marx's account, humanity proceeds along similar lines.[24]

Rand, in contrast, sees the mind as actively engaging the world, reaching out to grasp it, not passively responding to it. So human beings as such—not just communists, as in Marx—can escape their limited, historically conditioned understanding or reality. They can grasp fundamental, stable principles in various disciplines of the study of different spheres of reality, including in the sphere of political economy. As long as human nature exists—as long as there are bona fide human beings, something that is ascertainable by studying the world—certain ethical and political principles will be applicable to their lives; we can gradually, in good time, grasp these principles and implement them; but we might not—sometimes we may do it well, at others we might miss a great deal (so that the Ancient Greeks and the American Founders grasp it more or less well enough, while others failed to do so). For Rand, ironically again, one can be genuinely politically correct, while for Marxists and their philosophical brethren that is really impossible, because there will always be some new principles of political life that will supersede those currently "true."

In general terms, then, Ayn Rand has been perhaps the one major critic of Marxism who affirmed (against it) what Marx himself directly rejected and wanted the world to reject, namely, the individualist capitalist order. Yet Rand was not as hostile to Marx as some might believe. She found Marx more congenial, because of his secularism and naturalism, than another one of Marx's critics whose prominence and anti-communism is praised both on the left and the right, namely, Alexander Solzhenitsyn. Rand has criticized Solzhenitsyn for wanting to lead Russia into a period of anti-modernism, one that would rekindle the era of serfdom and mindlessness one associates with some of the most deeply religious epochs of human history. In contrast to that, one might suppose Rand thought, Marx was a liberator.

What Rand should be remembered for in connection with communism is her profoundly philosophical answer to Marx's ideas. If

Marx is secularism's greatest defender of collectivism, Ayn Rand is its greatest champion of individualism. And this individualism, unlike those heretofore, is not plagued by narrowness and severe paradox, such as the one we were provided by Hobbes and his followers.

Whether the reigning intelligentsia will ever honor Rand for her achievement remains a question. Too many today would have to eat their earlier words in favor of one type of collectivism or another. Too many are still hard at work resurrecting some version of the collectivist dream—via "market socialism," "democratic socialism," or "communitarianism."[25] Rand still stands as the most serious radical thinker who, maybe with a little help from her philosophical supporters, could effectuate a lasting challenge of 2,500 years of group think in our world, a kind of social philosophy that to our day hasn't stopped producing some of the most vile, catastrophic results for human community life. It may be most appropriate, therefore, to have the last word in this comparison between her and Karl Marx, recent history's most-often-invoked political philosopher. Here is perhaps the essence of Rand's political thought:

I am neither foe nor friend to my brothers, but such as each of them shall deserve of me. And to earn my love, my brothers must do more than to have been born. I do not grant my love without reason, nor to any chance passerby who may wish to claim it. I honor men with my love. But honor is a thing to be earned.

I shall choose friends among men, but neither slaves nor masters. And I shall choose only such as please me, and them I shall love and respect, but neither command nor obey. And we shall join our hands when we wish, or walk alone when we so desire. For in the temple of his spirit, each man is alone. Let each man keep his temple untouched and undefiled. Then let him join hands with others if he wishes, but only beyond his holy threshold.[26]

Endnotes

1   The contrast between the ancient and modern viewpoints is discussed by, among many others, Leo Strauss, *Natural Right and History*, 2nd ed. (Chicago: University of Chicago Press, 1972).

2   I thank David Kelley for reminding me of this point of similarity and difference between Rand and Marx.

³   Karl Marx, *Selected Writings*, ed., David McLellan (London: Oxford University Press, 1970), p. 126.

⁴   L. D. Easton and K. H. Guddat, eds. and trans., *Writings of the Young Marx on Philosophy and Society* (Garden City, N.Y.: Anchor Books, 1967), p. 39. This passage must be kept clearly in mind as one assesses Marx's view of values, including his conception of the good society. Marx's position is, indeed, reactionary — it is but a secular rendition of Western religions whereby we must be altruists through and through — not just benevolent, generous, and charitable on some occasions — in order to fulfill our moral mission, and wherein dualism prevails between our biological and our species being. See, in this connection, Tibor R. Machan, "Socialism as Reactionism," in K. Leube and A. Zlabinger, eds., *The Political Economy of Freedom: Essays in Honor of F. A. Hayek* (Munich, Germany: Philosophia Verlag, 1984), pp. 45-50

⁵   Karl Marx, *Grundrisse* (New York: Harper Torchbooks, 1977), p. 39.

⁶   H. B. Acton, *What Marx Really Said* (Atlantic Highlands, NJ: Humanities Press, 1967). Marx says "The individual and the species-life of man are not different...." Op. cit., *Selected Writings*, p. 91.

⁷   While Rand was no nominalist individualist, such as Hobbes and his neoclassical followers in economic science, she did endorse a form of metaphysical individualism whereby what exists in the world are individual beings, not, ultimately, concrete universals. See the discussion of this in Tibor R. Machan, *Individuals and Their Rights* (LaSalle, IL: Open Court., 1989), Chapter 1.

⁸   Karl Marx, *Das Kapital*, Chapter 1, fn. 15: "My standpoint, from which the evolution of the economic formation of society is viewed as a process of natural history, can less than any other make the individual responsible for relations whose creature he socially remains, however much he may subjectively raise himself above them." Op. cit., *Selected Writings*, p. 417. This "economic formation of society," it must be recalled, is the foundation of human life — the crux of Marx's economic determinism.

⁹   See Op. cit., Hardie, "The Final Good in Aristotle's Ethics."

¹⁰   This position is well developed in David L. Norton, *Personal Destinies, A Philosophy of Ethical Individualism* (Princeton, NJ: Princeton University Press, 1976). Rand develops her ideas in this ethical realm in her *The Virtue of Selfishness, A New Concept of Egoism* (New York: New American Library, 1961). See the previous chapter for more on this.

¹¹   See note 4 above.

¹²   See Marx's famous essay "On the Jewish Question," op. cit., *Selected Writings*. Marxists have continued to link such atomism with some justification to the classical liberal social philosophy, at least if they focus only on the economic analysis of capitalism.

¹³   It is in the neoclassical economic tradition that this legacy is most evident, including the two public policy divisions of that tradition, the public choice and law and economics schools. For more, see Tibor R. Machan, *Capitalism and Indi-*

vidualism, Reframing the Argument of the Free Society (New York: St. Martin's Press, 1990).

14   See Ludwig von Mises, *Human Action* (New Haven, CT: Yale University Press, 1949); F. A. Hayek, *The Constitution of Liberty* (Chicago: University of Chicago Press, 1961); Milton Friedman, *Capitalism and Freedom* (Chicago: University of Chicago Press, 1962), Robert Nozick, *Anarchy, State, and Utopia* (New York: Basic Books, 1974). (Nozick, in this work, joins utilitarians only in his subjectivism, whereby the meaning our life has must be given to it by us. In his later work, *The Examined Life* [New York: Simon and Schuster, 1991], Nozick repudiates his radical libertarianism.)

15   F.A. Hayek, *The Road to Serfdom* (Chicago: University of Chicago Press, 1944), p. 136.

16   Op. cit., *Ayn Rand's Marginalia*, p. 155.

17   Consider, for example, Milton Friedman. He defends free market capitalism on grounds that it best accommodates the self or private interests of its population. And he says, "The *private interest* is whatever it is that drives an individual" (Milton Friedman, "The Line We Dare Not Cross," *Encounter*, November 1976, p. 11). That is a typical characterization of human action by prominent economists. Ludwig von Mises argues that we act because some unease in our consciousness drives us to do so. He then invokes this idea as his major support for free market capitalism. See Ludwig von Mises, *Human Action* (New Haven, CT: Yale University Press, 1949), p. 69.

18   Rand's *Atlas Shrugged* was ranked second only to *The Bible* as the most popular book in the United States of America, in a 1990 survey by the Book of the Month Club.

19   Books on Rand have been authored mostly by admirers, past associates, and philosophical students of her thinking. The elite of the literary community have scoffed at her for her political views and have not bothered to analyze her writing, let alone her insightfulness about political matters. If there is anyone who has been uniformly politically incorrect during her life time, it has been Ayn Rand. It is not for nothing that Camille Paglia, the enfant terrible of anti-feminism, is compared to Rand by Paglia's critics and friends alike. A good example of a pejorative work is James T. Baker, *Ayn Rand* (Boston, MA: Twayne Publishers, 1987).

20   For a serious philosophical reading of this work, see Valerie Loiret-Prumet, "Ayn Rand and Feminist Synthesis: Rereading *We the Living*," in Mimi Reisel Gladstein and Chris Matthew Sciabarra, eds., *Feminist Interpretations of Ayn Rand* (Pennsylvania State University Press, 1998),

21   For biographical details on Rand, see Barbara Branden, *The Passion of Ayn Rand* (Garden City, NY: Doubleday, 1986). For some of the philosophical and literary themes, see Ronald E. Merrill, *The Ideas of Ayn Rand* (LaSalle, IL: Open Court, 1991).

22   To link individual liberty—or, more precisely, the legal system that protects the right of every individual to liberty of thought and action—and human crea-

tivity is not to disparage cooperative creative efforts, contrary to what contemporary communitarians and socio-economists have tended to maintain. (See, for example, Thomas A. Spragens, Jr., "The Limitations of Libertarianism," *The Responsive Community* [Winter and Spring 1992].) It is, however, to realize that such efforts will succeed if and only if the various participants individually choose to partake of and are not coerced into it.

[23] "Organic whole" is McLellan's translation, while "organic body" is preferred by others.

[24] I discuss these points of Marxism in more details in my *Marxism: A Bourgeois Critique* (Bradford, England: MCB University Press, 1988).

[25] The current revisionist trend in the United States of America, of introducing collectivism via the benign-sounding label "communitarianism," is led by Amitai Etzioni. See, for examples, his book *The Spirit of Community* (New York: Crown, 1993). For communitarianism to triumph as a social philosophy, however, it is evidently necessary to distort the true nature of individualism by caricaturing it in terms used mainly by positivist, neo-Hobbesian economists. See op. cit., Spragens, "The Limitations of Libertarianism," wherein nearly all the claims made about the nature of classical liberal politics are false, most importantly the idea that this social philosophy "fails to 'see' the legitimate role that moral equality, fellow feeling, and obligation play in a good democratic society." In fact the classical liberal tradition, most notably Rand's works, points clearly to the view that only when community and fellow feeling are not coerced can they reap positive results instead of mostly tyrannize the citizenry. (*The Responsive Community* is edited by Amitai Etzioni.) For more, see Aeon Skoble, "Another Caricature of Libertarianism," *Reason Papers*, No. 17 (Fall, 1992), pp. 107-112.

[26] Op. cit., *Anthem*, p. 111. I wish to thank Mark Turiano and David Kelley for their criticisms of an earlier draft of this chapter.

Chapter 6:
Rand's Moriarty

In the midst of a seminar attended by many students of Ayn Rand's thought, the question was raised as to why Rand found Immanuel Kant so detestable. The response, from a lecturer at this event, a professor of economics, was that Rand was simply ignorant. But that is not true. It will be useful to explore why Rand thought that Immanuel Kant was an evil person, not just philosophically mistaken.

The matter of Rand versus Kant has been a topic of discussion for some time, at least among those who find both thinkers important enough to study. There is little doubt that Kant is one of the most ambitious philosophers of the modern, post-Cartesian period of Western philosophy. He is also taken very seriously among contemporary philosophers, especially in ethics and epistemology, more so perhaps than even Aristotle.

When I was told of the response to the student's inquiry about why Rand is so critical of Kant, I thought that something better could be expected than the quip about Rand's ignorance. I would have expected at least a reasonable guess, some kind of inference from what one should know about Rand if one is willing to answer a question like that. In light of the frequency that this issue comes up in libertarian circles, it may be worthwhile to say a few helpful words about the topic.

The reason Rand detested Kant, if we go by what she actually thinks about the same topics Kant has discussed at great length, is that Kantian philosophy, as usually understood and interpreted by most who inquire about his ideas, is the most thorough, brilliant, devastating critique of human reason ever advanced in Western thought. Kant is usually taken to have argued that what the human mind understands the world to be is not the world *as it is* but *as it is made evident* to a particularly structured human reasoning faculty. Some argue that this is version of Kant is wrong—he only held that what the human mind understands is every bit as much an aspect of the world as anything can be, only a lot remains hidden from us, as well, whenever we try to figure things out. Indeed, some of Kant's writings published posthumously suggest this latter, unfamiliar way of taking Kant's views. Rand understood Kant in the first, standard version.[1]

Kant argued that the human mind's constitution — its nature — limits it from knowing whether its awareness (that is, its primary work of cognition) can produce knowledge of reality itself. Perhaps it is — but many believe that Kant argued we would never be able to make sure. Knowing that we know is not possible. There is the distinct prospect that the mind itself distorts reality for us. We can only be sure that we can "know" reality as it appears to us but not as it is in fact.

Kant seemed to think this is so because in the one area in which he thought bona fide knowledge of reality (in itself) could be attained, namely, about the nature of the human mind, he distinguished sharply between the knowledge we gain via science and the knowledge obtained from critical philosophy. Accordingly, the rest of reality — where all we have in the way of awareness is what science gives us via our possibly slanted human perspective — could very well be something other than what we understand it to be. And there is no way for us to check this, since we must check with our minds, the source of the trouble in the first place.

Rand found this outrageous. In her discussion of Paul Feyerabend's theory that science would be better if it were carried out without reference to any empirical or factual content,[2] Rand makes the following comment:

> "Science without Experience" heralds the retrogression of philosophy to the primordial, pre-philosophical rationalism of the jungle ("as was done only a few centuries ago," states the author, in support of a non-observational language). But what is innocent and explicable in an infant or a savage becomes senile corruption when the snake oil, totem poles and magic potions are replaced by a computer. This is the sort of rationalism that Plato, Descartes and all the others of that school would be ashamed of; but not Kant. This is his baby and his ultimate triumph, since he is the most fertile father of the doctrine equating the means of consciousness with its content — I refer you to his notion that the machinery of consciousness produces its own (categorial) content.[3]

Rand, in turn, is perhaps the most ardent advocate ever of the efficacy of human rationality to know reality exactly as it is. As we have seen, Rand considers "concepts ... the products of a mental process that integrates and organizes the evidence provided by man's senses."[4] In contrast, she understands Kant to have advocated that concepts are constructed, based on certain inherent features of human consciousness. By this Kantian understanding, Rand claims, religion, science, and philosophy are all on equal footing as far as their truth is concerned.[5]

Rand clearly thought that Kant was the Moriarty to her Aristotelian Sherlock Holmes — the supremely brilliant, evil destroyer. It made not a whit of difference to Rand that in some areas, such as some parts of moral philosophy and in politics, Kant was closer to her own ideas than are most other philosophers. For example, Kant stressed principled conduct and defended the sovereignty of the individual's free will, just as he supported a largely liberal legal order. He did stress the idea of every person being "an end in himself," an expression that Rand clearly makes welcome use of.

But these were not fundamental matters to Rand. Kant's fundamental doubts about the human mind's capacity to know reality as it really is just could not be forgiven. How could a brilliant man make such perverse use of argument, the major tool of his own mind? How could he subscribe to such a grand paradox: We cannot know that we ever truly know reality? Not only is this highly paradoxical, since that knowledge would then be impossible for Kant to produce. It is also an affront not only to human achievements of all kinds through history but, especially, to the possibility of sound philosophical work.

Rand concluded, I believe, that Kant had to do some fundamental evading and was out to accomplish a not so hidden agenda, namely, to vindicate the Christian faith as a substitute for confident metaphysical knowledge.

But there is at least one point Rand probably overlooked, namely, that Kant did his work in an intellectual climate of mechanistic materialism. Without introducing a realm or aspect of reality apart from that which the science of his days studied, there would have been no justification at all for accepting that human beings have a moral nature: free will and moral responsibility. Mechanistic materialism leaves no room for morality, and Kant knew this.

Many contemporary libertarians — especially those who work in the social sciences such as economics — find Rand's ideas, including the stress on ethics, natural rights, and so one, incredible for the same reason: science appears to contradict such notions. Kant was firmly convinced, however, that human beings are moral agents. And it appears that the only way he could make this intellectually palatable is by grafting on to the "scientific" view of his day the skeptical philosophical ideas that denied that scientific view full authority. It may not have been mysticism or religion, per se, that Kant wanted to bolster but the moral realm of human life, albeit his solution fell short of being adequate.[6]

Rand herself solves the problem, roughly, by discrediting the model of knowledge (absolute, timeless certainty, certainty beyond a shadow of doubt) that Kant invoked as the ideal; by recasting the conception of the knowing mind itself as metaphysically inactive but active only epistemically—as a tool or faculty for grasping but not for molding reality, as it were—and thus incapable of interfering with what it knows or understands; by rejecting the mechanistic view of science and thus making ample room for a self-determining, free agent such as human beings seem to be (see, for more on this, Roger W. Sperry's popular and technical work,[7] and Dennis Senchuk's defense of a non-reductionist conception of human consciousness[8]); and by rejecting the radical empiricism of Hume, et al., which seem to require that the "is" of the famous problem of deriving an "ought" from an "is," have no content other than pure sense data and that the relations of logic must all be formally deductive.

Some of these controversies still plague the broad classical liberal/libertarian arena of philosophy, ethics, and politics. Rand was of course characteristically fervent about how to make the case for something she regarded as sensible and true, and she found Kant's efforts to be full of pitfalls, indeed, morally deplorable, comparable to an artist whose task is to destroy art.

Was Rand then justified in morally deriding and detesting Immanuel Kant? I don't think so, but neither can I say she was not. That would depend on more in-depth knowledge of Kant the person than I have. I don't know whether Rand had such knowledge. I doubt it.

Endnotes

1   For an academic philosopher who deals with these issues at great length and who understands Kant as Rand did, see Edward Pols, *Radical Realism* (Ithaca, NY: Cornell University Press, 1998).

2   Paul Feyerabend, "Science Without Experience," *Journal of Philosophy*, November 20, 1969, pp.

3   Ayn Rand, *Philosophy: Who Needs It* (Indianapolis, IN: Bobbs-Merrill Company, Inc., 1982), pp. 106-7.

4   Ibid., p. 108.

5   Ibid., pp. 93-94. Interestingly, Rand's belief that Kant was much more a mystic than a philosopher of reason, as many believe, has recently gained support from the work of Gregory R. Johnson, a graduate of The Catholic University of America, whose dissertation, "A Commentary on Kant's *Dreams of a Spirit-Seer*," argues for a strong connection between Kant and the Swedish mystic Emanuel Swedenborg. See, for more, Scott McLemee, "Under the Influence, The long Shadow of Emanuel Swedenborg," *Lingua Franca* (May/June 1998), pp. 58-61.

6   I leave this judgment unsupported here except to say that any kind of dualism of the sort we find in Kant leaves unanswered the basic issue of how the two realms manage to interact — why do some thoughts, for example, give one goose bumps? More importantly, how does a conviction or judgment manage to prompt behavior?

7   Roger W. Sperry, *Science and Moral Priority* (New York: Columbia University Press, 1983).

8   Dennis Senshuk, "Consciousness Naturalized," *The American Philosophical Quarterly* , January 1991.

Chapter 7:
Room for Work

Some Objections Considered

Ayn Rand was no academic philosopher and her scholarship, involving the customary dialogues in which professional academics take part, was minimal. She did, on occasion, take up the works of certain academic thinkers — B.F. Skinner and, indirectly, John Rawls, as well as more friendly adversaries such as John Herman Randall, Ludwig von Mises, and Brand Blanshard.

Despite her absence from the intellectual hustle-bustle of academic scholarship, Rand's writings have inspired a good deal of philosophical reflection, at least among some who entered the discipline after she had made her contributions. She has not been well received, however, by communitarians, conservatives, and skeptics. Rand is certainly not in line with those who cherish the classical liberal tendency toward embracing value subjectivism.

Rand regarded Objectivism a philosophical system and she was eager to stress that it is not her conclusions in ethics and politics that makes Objectivism sound. It is the foundations that lead to the defense of the individual and to individual liberty. In the area of applied ethics Rand's view is unique because it tends to support opposition to any kind of government intrusion on the lives and property of individuals, without embracing the position of such libertarians as Tristan Engelhardt and Robert Nozick (when he wrote *Anarchy, State, and Utopia*). In short, Rand does not fend off government intervention and regulation because she holds that no one can know what is right and good. Instead she holds that people have basic rights to liberty because they must choose freely to pursue the good life, to do the right thing, something that's possible to do.

Let us consider now academic philosopher Norman Barry, who addressed Rand's ideas directly in his book *Classical Liberalism and Libertarianism*.[1]

Teleology

First let us focus on Barry's characterization of Rand's political ideas, although this will require that we also take into consideration certain points Rand makes in other branches of philosophy.

Let me begin with Barry's claims (on page 110) that "the rationale of those *constraints* on individual action which an organized capitalist society requires...does not have to rest on any particular teleology." This is supposed to be an objection to the Objectivist idea that an understanding of human nature is required so as to develop a sound moral and political understanding, and what such an understanding gives us is that human beings are purposive beings, with a *telos* or end inherent in their nature, namely, their happiness. As Aristotle believed, for example, each human being has a natural desire to know — meaning that it would be in the nature of every person to benefit from knowledge and understanding.

Barry does not explain what he means by "teleology." It means, in fact, the examination of a conception of the end or goal of various beings. With reference to human life, it studies the purpose of it supposed by proponents to be identifiable by reference to human nature.

Rand distinguishes between any possible telos in nature and the purposive goal directedness of human action:

> When applied to physical phenomena, such as the automatic functions of an organism, the term 'goal-directed' is not to be taken to mean 'purposive' (a concept applicable only to the actions of a consciousness) and is not to imply the existence of any teleological principle operating in insentient nature. I use the term 'goal-directed,' in this [meta-ethical] context, to designate the fact that the automatic functions of living organisms are actions whose nature is such that they result in the preservation of an organism's life.[2]

For Rand, then, purposiveness exists only for human beings. Teleological phenomena may occur in the rest of living nature, while neither purpose nor telos exists in insentient nature. Goal-directedness occurs in the living world because all living organisms act in such ways as to produce a result that furthers their survival and flourishing — that "they result in the preservation of an organism's life."

For Rand, everyone has a human nature, which means being a thinking, rational, and purposive animal. Being rational involves determining the ends of one's life in a coherent fashion, based on the facts one learns about oneself and reality. Therefore, each person is to lead his or her own life cogently, realizing potentials, developing talents, fulfilling likes, in ways that can proceed without inherent conflict or inconsistency.

Further Reflections on Rights

Now, in contrast to Rand, Norman Barry seems to hold that a theory of individual rights ("constraints") does not have to rest on some given understanding of human goal-directed biology, not to mention a purposive conception of human conscious life.

In response to this it is worth considering whether there can be constraints on what others may do *to us* even though there is nothing in particular we ought to do with ourselves? If we have no sound purpose to serve in our lives why should there be any prohibition on others to use us to serve their purposes? Even on Barry's view, at least one purpose would have to be granted or proper for everyone, namely, to respect the constraints that characterize classical liberal society's basic principles. But, why grant Barry's constraints if there is nothing of significance to be protected by such constraints?

In any case, Barry does not show that one can defend individual rights without recourse to some theory of what human beings ought to do with their lives. When Barry explains (pp. 124-125) Rand's attempt to connect doing the right things with having rights, he does not mention a most crucial element of doing right—it needs to be done as a matter of choice or volition.

While Rand makes clear that it is *"right* for [a human being] to think," Barry does not note the crucial point in the next clause, namely, "it is *right* to act on his own free judgment."[3] So even if one were to do the wrong thing, since it is right for one to act on one's own free judgment, others would be wrong to prohibit one to act as one judges (however wrong one in fact is).[4]

Barry is also wrong to think that it is "not difficult to see how an individualist teleology may become a collectivist one." The term "may" is very loose—of course, some persons may think that an individualist teleology may modulate over time into a collectivist one. But not because the logic of the concepts permits it. Certainly, Barry does not bother to back up this suggestion.

Even if it is true, so what? Rand is not talking about just any "individualist teleology" but a teleological individualism, one that has as one of its most basic tenets that every human being is a moral agent and to achieve the proper moral objectives of his or her life, *each* person in society requires moral space (Nozick's term)—i.e., a determinate sphere of inviolate individual jurisdiction (secured through the institution of the principle of the right to private property).

Skepticism and Rights Theory

Barry refers to Rand (p. 111) as if she would accept the characterization of human thinking as "potentially infallible." But "infallible" means "incapable of making a mistake." And Rand has no illusions about human beings ever managing to guarantee against mistakes. They are clearly capable of engaging in mistaken, fallacious, or evasive reasoning.

Rand holds not that reason is potentially infallible but that despite its being fallible, we need not make mistakes—it isn't *necessarily* failing. In other words, from the mere fact that reason has gone wrong before, it does not follow (indeed, it is impossible to argue correctly) that it will/must go wrong again. It *might*, of course, since reason is a faculty that *can* err. But this is merely to observe a capacity, not to have any clue as to whether that capacity is going to be fulfilled or unfulfilled on any given occasion.

Skepticism (especially about ethics) of the sort apparently championed by Barry (e.g., Hume, Hayek) involves the logical mistake of inferring from past mistakes the impossibility of getting things right. Yet there is no logic in this—just because you have in the past made errors in addition, it does not follow that you must or even will be making an error today. Nor could we know, were such a skepticism true, that a mistake had been made in the past, since that would require confidence in some claim to knowledge, namely, that one which rectified the past mistake and showed it up to be a mistake.

Barry also seems convinced that from moral skepticism one can derive a case for individual rights. He does not appreciate, though, just how deeply such skepticism cuts—as far as individual rights. If we cannot know ethical truths, we could not know about individual rights or any political constraints that obligate one to abstain from acting in certain (intrusive) ways—i.e., if skepticism is correct, how could we know that persons *ought not to* impose themselves upon the lives of others without permission and may be fended off when they do so? Why does this norm not fall by the tenets of skepticism?

Now, admittedly, this is no argument for anything but it surely makes it evident why someone like Ayn Rand thinks it imperative that moral knowledge be securable—without it the case for the free society falls apart. Nor is it enough *to pretend* that we had moral knowledge—once the news is out that it is just a ruse, the edifice built on it will fall to pieces and nihilism shall commence.

Rand's Alleged Rationalism

It is, furthermore, wrong to label Rand a rationalist—that means someone who proposes to derive all truths from first principles *alone* and usually by merely thinking them up in the unaided human mind (as per Descartes, Spinoza)!

For example, nowhere does Rand claim that "We know *a priori* that all events have a cause." This is Barry's imposition of a view on Rand that she rejects—she is, as we have already seen, neither an empiricist nor a rationalist.

Rand does hold that "the law of causality is the law of identity applied to action," meaning that the fact of X being I (having this identity) will necessarily condition the way X will interact with the surrounding world, something that isn't true a priori—based on some pre-experiential understanding—but on the plain fact that nothing can be produced by nothing. (In other words, when X is a, b and c and a, b, and c can produce x, y, and z but not p, q, and r, this is because results other than p, q and r would have no source—they would simply pop into existence.)

Thus, Rand would hold, that a hammer enables us to make a dent in a car's fender but a softly spoken word will not. Our understanding of hammers and cars and dents provides us with this knowledge. (And the "necessity" involved is the realistic—not fantastic or so-called "logical"—necessity of all scientific-engineering claims.) Similarly, given what a human being is, force will not produce morally good behavior but personal resolve can do this.

Certainly, our engineering sciences rest on such facts of reality, rather than on some supposed contingency that Barry thinks obtains.

Our political and other social sciences, in turn, are going astray—rational analysis is precluded from them—because they fail to heed the point.

Rand adheres to a pluralistic conception of what there is and thus of how we might come to know it. The simplistic division of the world into the empirical and the rational sectors is alien to Rand's way of thinking. Barry's efforts to use the division to classify Rand's views just will not succeed in those terms. Indeed, by the common sense (as distinct from radical) understanding of "empirical," Rand takes the law of causality as an empirical principle—i.e., a principle of how the world actually works discovered in part by the utilization of one's sensory organs.

For Barry and Co., however, "empirical" means, most significantly, contingent, i.e., a state of affairs that does not have to be so and might just be otherwise—anytime, anywhere. Contingent used to mean, in philosophy, "dependent upon the will of God." When God became unfashionable, it was retained to mean "conditional and not necessary, could be otherwise, not having to be the case or "not logically impossible." But all this is dependent heavily upon a very rich and questionable theory in terms of which, for example, "certainty" came to mean "incorrigible," "infallible," "true beyond a shadow of a doubt." Once one accepts this theory and its language, there is no telling what else you must buy into and usually it leads (logically) to the conviction we find in Paul Feyerabend and Richard Rorty, namely, that every belief is equally good and we must leave it all up to small democratic assemblies or "our" communities to decide what will prevail. It recalls the old Greek thinker, Cratylus, who stopped talking because he realized that talk assumes some measure of consistency of meaning of terms over time, and skeptics are not entitled to this.

Causality

Moreover, Barry chides Rand (on page 114) as follows: "how men can make the best use of their resources cannot be answered directly from the laws of logic." But Rand never makes any claim from which one could infer the view that the laws of logic alone will guide one to make the best use of one's resources. This is the kind of attribution that one can expect of Feyerabend, who loves to needle his opponents regardless of what is true, since all truth for him is perspectival. Should we infer from Barry's choice of such a strategy of criticism that he also has no regard for truth and accuracy? Or does it simply show his ignorance—or his disdain? In any case, it misses the mark by a wide margin.

For Rand the law of causality is a substantive metaphysical fact of reality—the law is the fact that the actions of any being must have determinate consequences (what one would ordinarily term "cause and effect") because entities are going to make their impact on their surroundings and elsewhere in terms of what these entities are. Anything else would, as noted above, violate the principle that nothing can come from nothing, a principle that skeptics, of course, find unsupported because one can imagine otherwise. (Recall, for example, David Hume's disparagement of the principle.)

Certainty

Barry also goes on to ascribe to Rand the idea of "dogmatic certainty," again without any justification. Indeed, one should notice how little of what Barry cites from Rand comes from her more organized philosophical writings—*Introduction to Objectivist Epistemology*. If he had consulted that, he could never have said, without some self-betrayal, that "Rand's epistemology is *authoritarian*" (p. 115). This is not to say that Rand, as many other thinkers with a great variety of beliefs, did not have something of an authoritarian personality. But so did Wittgenstein, Freud, Popper, and others, not to mention Feyerabend himself. (In contrast, the Platonist Leo Strauss was a gentle soul, indeed.)

Barry states, also, without any argument to back up the claim, that "it is not difficult to see how a collectivist ethic could be deduced from certain premises asserted to be *absolutely* true"(p. 116). But even if this is granted, what of it? Clearly, truths will help us know more truths. So given certain premises, no doubt we will derive conclusions from them. And some of these conclusions will be collectivist, some not, depending on the premises.

I believe Rand would argue against Barry that he makes the mistake of thinking that anyone can escape all premises that in effect function as absolutely true in their viewpoint. There is no such thing as "It's turtles all the way." After all, without some basic premise—

signifying a basic fact—say, about the function of absolutist premises, how would anyone be able to draw any conclusions that could serve as something of a stable ground for any conclusion, let alone for personal or political conduct?[5]

Consider, if we don't know it is right to respect rights—to respect personal autonomy or sovereignty—why *should* we respect these? If a gun-toting hood demands your money and you say, "You cannot know whether you ought to take my money," why is this any objection to his taking the money anyway? He can say, "I don't know either, but I wish to take it, so I will, especially since you haven't got any well-grounded objections to offer against my doing so."

I have never been able to understand why some classical liberals and libertarians rest so much hope with skepticism. Furthermore, skeptics such as Sartre, Feyerabend, Rorty, John Gray, Shirley Robin Letwin, et al. have indeed endorsed numerous anti-libertarian measures.

Normative Features of a Free Society as per Ayn Rand

For Rand, two elements of morality are crucial: that there can be an objective good, and that each person is free to choose between the good and its alternatives. If there is no objective good, it is impossible to guide one's conduct intelligently, cogently—it is rudderless. If there is no choice, one is not in the position to be guiding one's life at all, so what is good or bad becomes irrelevant. Indeed, that much is contained in the famous Kantian motto, namely, "ought implies (or presupposes) can." It requires that choice be possible, as well as that there be some standards by which to choose the right thing. If one lacks either of these preconditions, morality—including all the shoulds and oughts of classical liberals—is voided.

Barry notes (p. 129) that Rand combines the goal-setting and the knowledge integrative function of human reason. And why not—as I noted earlier, Aristotle observed that "All men by nature desire to know." That is to say, the proper course by his or her nature of everyone is to set out to know. So the proper goal of every human being is to know and to act on the knowledge he or she obtains. "Focus" is the moral exclamation that comes from the Rand's egoistic ethics. It is basic to the human self that it is made the best it can be—that it will benefit itself most—via the conscientious employment of reason.

Finally, Barry repeats the claim that "deontological principles (those that would forbid someone being used on behalf of another) ... hold independently of any ends or purposes that reason might be said to prescribe"(page 130). He does not defend this claim at this point, so it is difficult to see why its support of liberty would be more successful than Rand's. More importantly, it seems clearly to be false—as I argued at the outset. Why not use another if he has no use for himself? He'd go to waste! Deontology without the substance of *telos* lacks a compass, while *telos* without the constrains of deontology is licentious.

This does not exhaust what one might fruitfully say about Norman Barry's discussion of Objectivism in his chapter, "Ayn Rand and Egoism." But this much will have indicated how Rand might respond to Barry's criticism.

On Axiomatic Concepts and Propositions
In the case of Rand's ideas on axiomatic concepts and propositions, we may call on several works, some treating Rand's ideas quite directly, others addressing the same topic. Since this is such a crucial aspect of Rand's outlook—she would fully agree to that—criticisms of it will be considered prior to turning to the less basic issues in Rand's philosophy.

I want to examine contemporary objections to the Aristotelian-Randian approach. Before doing so, however, I must step back and take stock of what is going on here.

I will be examining a number of objections to the (Principle of Non-Contradiction). I will spell it out again and make use of Rand's or Aristotle's method of demonstrating it by refutation.

The PNC is a signal example of a philosophical principle. All objections to it are themselves philosophical in nature, or at least philosophical in import. They emerge from within a philosophical position. But what is it to have such a position? And what does the nature of a philosophical position allow us to conclude about these objections to the PNC?

My first clue is that all philosophers criticize other philosophers or philosophical views. What does such criticism presuppose? First, it presupposes that the critics and the criticized exist and share enough of a common world for communication to take place. Second, it presupposes that the parties to the dialogue are conscious of one another and of their positions. Third, it presupposes that the critics and the criticized are different. If they are not different individuals – as, for example, in a thought-experiment – then they are at least different aspects of the same individual.

A second clue is that even those who deny the PNC must employ arguments and whatever arguments presuppose (e.g., logic). The frequent critical discussions engaged in by those who make such denials presuppose some (at least implicit) commitment to logic, however eagerly this commitment may ultimately be denied. The very act of denying the PNC could not mean anything without the prior acceptance of the binding character of what is being denied. Even the most vehement proponents of ontological relativity assume certain standards. What, after all, could be the (rational) force of criticism based upon standards that do not have a status over and above convention, temporary interest, subjective preference, or sheer whim?[6] The criticisms leveled by relativist philosophers frequently purport to deliver a knock-out punch. In virtue of what? And indeed, it does appear that something firm – at least as firm as a political agenda – is being hinted at in advancing even the most relativist or irrationalist views.

But do not these preliminary observations alone secure for us what Aristotle had in mind, namely the ontological status of the PNC? Do they not secure for us what Rand had in mind, namely the truth of her philosophical axioms? To confirm this, let us consider some concrete examples.

O'Neill's Skepticism about the PNC

William F. O'Neill argues against Rand's view that the PNC is undeniable, so fundamental that it cannot be dispensed with, regardless on how much one may try. This is how O'Neill addresses this issue:

> If...I am sincere, and my stated rejection of the law of contradiction is the last sensible statement which I choose to make (since all normal discourse is based on logical assumptions), I cannot be accused of being self-contradictory because I abstain from all subsequent attempts to rationalize or defend my illogicality. In such a case, of course, my assertion that I reject the formal law of contradiction will be a terminal assertion. I have now quit playing the logic-game of true-false dichotomies altogether.... My choice is

to live without considering the idea at all, let us say, intuitively at a purely spontaneous (pre-verbal) level of response in something approximating Zen awareness.[7]

First of all, note that O'Neill construes the kind of contradiction involved in denying the PNC as a contradiction between propositions, whereas in fact it is a contradiction between a proposition and the ontological conditions of asserting the proposition. Second, to the extent that O'Neill's "Zen awareness" allows life to go on in a "spontaneous" and intuitive—though "pre-verbal"—manner, he falls victim to Aristotle's rebuttal of Cratylus' gambit of shutting up and pointing. This objection can be extended to those who give up propositional speech not only for pointing, but for grunting, commands, and various other "intuitive" or "spontaneous" non-propositional ways of signifying.

Even if one indicates something with a grunt, one is indicating this as opposed to that. One is registering the phenomena of difference and determinateness, which are the foundation of the PNC. If O'Neill were simply to gesture mutely—for instance, pointing out items on a menu—then, presumably, he is indicating this entree rather than that entree. And, no doubt he would gesture in anger if the waiter brings him the wrong order. Clearly, then, he is aware of the determinacy and difference of things, which awareness, if put into speech, would be the PNC. Therefore, O'Neill tacitly admits the truth of what he denies to be the case in his (last) words. To the extent that O'Neill's "Zen awareness" approaches what Aristotle called a vegetative state of existence, it is a testament to the depths of self-stultifying absurdity to which contentiousness can bring us. It also testifies to a misunderstanding on O'Neill's part of the purpose of philosophical argument, which is not primarily to change the mind of any stubborn opponent, but to establish whether something is or is not the case. The fact that O'Neill's only escape from granting the ontological status of the PNC is to choose "to live without considering the idea at all" should be sufficient to establish the real point at issue: the rational unavoidability of the PNC.

It should be added that all critics of PNC stumble by failing to see that their communication—the very meaningfulness of what they say—rests, in part, on the PNC. The letters that they use, the sounds they make, must be what they are and cannot be not what they are, lest no communication be possible. In other words, the factuality of parts of speech — words, commas, letters, etc. — retain their constancy and can thus be used successfully for purposes of communication, because of the PNC.[8]

R. M. Dancy's Doubts About the PNC

R. M. Dancy, in an extensive study of Aristotle's position on the PNC, raises considerations that indirectly bear on Rand's position on axiomatic concepts and propositions:

> One might deny the law of non-contradiction for all sorts of reasons. None that I have seen strike me as good reasons. But neither do I see any reason for saying that there never could be good reason for denying it.[9]

Dancy's work explores the varied issues, pro and con, surrounding the Aristotelian stance. For the most part, his conclusions are sound. Still, he is wrong in this last skeptical reflection. Dancy is denying the universal scope of the PNC. He is willing to grant that, on the basis of enumerative induction, he has not seen a good reason to deny the PNC. But he is willing to entertain the possibility that some good reason might come along. But presumably such a good reason would refer to some matter of fact or some philosophical principle (which, ultimately, must derive its sense from some matter of fact). Presumably, this matter of fact must have some determinate content; it must be something. From Dancy's own words, we can know at least one thing about its determinate content: It is such that, if Dancy were to encounter it, it would be capable of persuading him to deny the PNC. Yet this involves a paradox. If it is determinate enough to persuade Dancy that it supports the denial of the PNC then it is determinate enough to be further evidence of the PNC. Again, the PNC is not valid just of the facts we can enumerate. It is true of all possible facts, including those Dancy considers to be possible counter-examples.

Yet even this Aristotelian response has been met with further skeptical objections to the effect that it simply carries no ontological import. All the self-refutation argument shows, these skeptics claim, is that those who engage in some form of verbal communication commit themselves to certain standards. But what if one decides to deny the PNC and then simply shuts up?

Nussbaum's Reservations

Martha Craven Nussbaum, in her provocative essay "Saving Aristotle's Appearances," maintains that Aristotle does not demonstrate that the PNC has an ontological status, but merely that it is unavoidable given the structure of our common, socially inculcated language and conceptual framework. Thus Aristotle's demonstration of the PNC by refutation merely testifies to his rootedness in the Greek form of life.[10]

The essential problem with Nussbaum's argument for the relativity of the PNC is that it is premised upon a fantastic idea of absolute truth. For Nussbaum, an absolute truth is external to our language and conceptual framework, and cannot be captured by them, for any such truths would become ipso facto "internal" and, therefore, relative. Since Nussbaum seems to identify consciousness with the linguistically relative or mediated, she is in effect arguing that absolute truths are precisely those truths of which we are not conscious. Now, whatever views of absolute truth have, I submit that this is not one of them.

Nussbaum is led to this position by her equivocal use of the concepts of what lies "inside" or "outside" of consciousness. Nussbaum accepts the traditional claim that absolute truths are in some sense "outside" of consciousness. But "outside" of consciousness is ambiguous. It can mean that the absolute object of consciousness exists independent of, but knowable by, consciousness. Or it can mean that the absolute object is outside of all relationship to consciousness, i.e., unknown. I submit that the defenders of absolute truth hold that their truths are "outside" of consciousness in the first sense, not the second sense. That is to say: an absolute truth is a truth that is known as absolute, a fact that has both entered into the grasp of consciousness and is grasped precisely as existing independent of the grasp of consciousness. Nussbaum, however, holds that absolutists mean the latter sense of "outside." Then, by identifying knowledge with being "inside" consciousness — being relative to our language or conceptual schemes — she saddles the absolutist with the absurd position of seeking absolute truth (truths lying outside of the grasp of consciousness) which, as soon as they are captured (brought into the grasp of consciousness), evaporate into relative truths by the mere fact of being known.

Another way of approaching this issue is through an ambiguity in the use of "inside." The absolutist may well be willing to grant that an absolute truth is somehow "internal" to our language and conceptual framework, for it is precisely through our language and conceptual framework that we grasp absolute truths. The trouble with this kind of language is that we are also constantly tempted to "locate" our language and conceptual schemes "inside" our minds, or even in our brains. The problem is this implies that if our world is "inside" our language and our language is "inside" our heads, then the world is located inside our heads, nested in Chinese boxes, as it were.

Yet this is an absurd position, reached by an equivocal use of the word "inside." In the first sense, "inside" means "mediated by." In the second, it means "located within." Thus, in order to avoid the problems posed by this ambiguity, the absolutist stresses that, however mediated or "inside" our knowledge is, it is still knowledge of something that exists outside—something not located in the head. Returning now to Aristotle, we may grant that for Aristotle the PNC is "inside"—that is, mediated by—our conceptual schemes. But once it comes "inside" our conceptual schemes, it is appreciated precisely as "outside" of them—as an objective, ontological truth.

Indeed, talk of "inside" and "outside" should not be taken very seriously, as if two realities existed corresponding to these two terms. All that "inside" means is that it is ourselves, our thinking and perceiving, that is at issue—the reality of these is no less a reality than of anything else. It just turns out that for us there is our (individual) awareness of whatever we are aware of and there is whatever our awareness makes evident to us, including our awareness itself.

Problems Left for Objectivism

If one considers Rand's Objectivism as her greatest achievement—as one would in the case of any philosopher that what he or she proposed as a set of philosophical solutions must be the ultimate test of merit—we can say this: Ayn Rand developed the broad outlines and some of the details of a complete philosophy which, however, is open-ended and allows for, indeed invites, continued development.

Rand's epistemological idea that definitions are open-ended makes this clear:

> ...when and if some discovery were to make [a] definition.... Inaccurate...would the question of expanding the definition arise. 'Expanding' does not mean negating, abrogating or contradicting; it means demonstrating that some other characteristics are more distinctive....
>
> Since man is not omniscient, a definition cannot be changelessly absolute, because it cannot establish the relationship of a given group of existents to everything else in the universe, including the undiscovered and unknown.[11]

Rand is a contextualist, holding that a true definition must be "*contextually* absolute" so that it must not fail to "specify the known relationship among existents (in terms of the known essential characteristics)" and that must not "contradict the known (by omission or evasion)."[12]

That a philosophy is conducive to further development, is quite possibly one of its assets. The future isn't known sufficiently. We aren't able to tell now that certain topics cannot be further discussed with profit. Also, philosophers, as the rest of us, often economize—few are as comprehensive as Plato, Aristotle, Spinoza, Kant, or Hegel. Nietzsche, Schopenhauer, or even Heidegger is only suggestive on such classical philosophical topics of truth, causality, free will, and justice.

Rand, whose major achievements are literary, left many philosophical topics—both in the fundamental branches and in special areas of her focus—undeveloped, even untreated. Because her work in philosophy aspires toward building a system, not content with bits and pieces of analysis, one may express some disappointment that she did not discuss issues that are crucial in the discipline. However, for the same reason, those who consider her basic outline to be very promising have good leads to advance to these other issues in ways Rand would welcome.

So what is there to develop in Objectivism?

Metaphysics

One of the most important issues in philosophy is how change comes about—for example, in the emergence of life from inanimate things (to pick on perhaps the most perplexing of problems and one that leads many serious thinkers to postulate God as a unique, even supernatural spiritual, incorporeal entity with the power to produce something as complex as the universe that seems to follow intelligible patterns and developments).

Rand disavowed materialism but often spoke in ways that suggested her thinking could be analyzed into a materialist framework. She considered perceptual awareness to be reliant on the fact that matter is perceived, nothing else. Yet there are serious problems about the very idea of matter—in physics there seems to be no such concept that is fundamental. Even by Rand's own account, matter has to be a something or other, a being that has identity, whereas in, for example, Aristotle, matter is without form or nature, so it cannot have identity. So by Rand's own account, it seems there is no matter as such, in the sense in which it is supposed to be some kind of primordial stuff without shape, form, nature. But then what is left of her claim that perception is aware of material reality? Does it help to change this to physical reality? It would not appear so, unless there exists a category or domain of being characterized by certain properties—mass, dimension, spatial location, or the like. But that could be said of matter, as well, in which case Rand would be a materialist and her disavowal of the mystics of muscle would be disingenuous.

It is perhaps possible to classify Rand as a naturalist, someone who takes reality or nature to be a whole system of beings united by some fundamental, axiomatic principles, leaving it open for further, scientific inquiry as to what is the exact nature of such beings. In that case, her account of perceptual knowledge would have to be taken very seriously—which is where the work of someone like David Kelly, in his *The Evidence of the Senses*,[13] comes in as a significant addition to the corpus of Objectivism. Yet it does not address metaphysical and ontological issues, which is where the difficulties arise.

The cosmological question of "the beginning of the universe," if one can even speak of the Big Bang and all its attendant theories this way, is another topic that Rand hardly touched upon. She did adhere to the principle of the conservation of matter-energy but disavowed materialism, which is often taken to be the basis of this principle. Rand's basis, though, appears to be more along lines that nothing can come from nothing—zero cannot turn into any unit, any existent—and the impossibility of something being totally annihilated. Indeed, this is one reason Rand is an atheist, since it is logically incoherent, as far as she sees it, that some being could have produced the natural world out of nothing natural but a supernatural event not involving the causal, productive processes that constitute natural changes studied by science.

The idea of God, for Rand, constituted "an insult to my intelligence," to quote her hero Howard Roark, mainly because it involved so many mind boggling attributes. Omnipotence, omniscience, omnibenevolence, for example, do not appear to be compatible with the existence of a world such as ours. Rand might have found W. Somerset Maugham's point agreeable that "I have little patience with the writers who try to reconcile in one conception the Absolute of the metaphysician with the God of Christianity. But if I had had any doubts, the [First World] war would have effectually silenced them."[14]

In Galt's speech Rand is especially disturbed about the idea of original sin, which she takes to mean that human beings are already guilty of a moral evil in infancy and thus dismisses as a monstrously unjust notion.[15] Some sophisticated theologians dispute this rendition, claiming that all that's meant by "original sin" is a capacity for moral vice. Yet this does not seem to jell easily with the ritual of baptism, which is a *cleansing* process. Why would one need it if one is only capable of sinning but needn't yet be sinful?

Epistemology

It is also important to work out just what the relationship is between a definition of a concept and the nature of what the concept means. For example, human beings are defined as "beings of volitional consciousness." Is there in some sense a referent for this definition in the world or is it a summary statement, a kind of place in a system of labels or designations. What, then, does the definition refer to in reality? And do these remain stable or can they change, just as the definitions can, albeit for different reasons? Is the grouping of attributes referred to in definitions itself justified by reference to facts of reality?

Rand considers concepts contextual, as we have seen. Valid concepts cannot be finished forever. They have to be the best we can achieve for the time being. From the past we learn that concepts grow. Yet suppose they grow extensively beyond what they mean now so that a concept "apple" means a specific range of beings now but in two million years it will be used differently, although correctly. Does this not suggest that our understanding is subjective, historically relative, and dependent upon our temporal position?

Rand did deal with this problem quite extensively in the appendix to her *Introduction to Objectivist Epistemology*. She was clearly aware of the threat.

In this connection we might also notice that many have raised the issue of whether there is sufficient room in Rand for spirituality. She does note that such a dimension of human life can be identified provided it refers to the valuational aspects of human consciousness — art, culture, ethics, politics, and so on. Yet there is a question about the existence of spirituality as an experiential primary, one spoken of by mystics (sometimes incessantly). As someone suggested, here is an experience a little like sexual climax — one knows what it is without really being able to tell another without that same kind of experience about it. Mystical experiences of that kind have been testified to and unless one is willing to dismiss the reports as complete fabrications, something needs to be taken account of that is being referred to here. Rand appears to be cavalierly dismissive of the idea rather than cautiously open-minded.

Rand's famous motto, "check your premises," is nice but not all that helpful because sometimes premises human beings invoke and work with are seriously hidden from awareness itself. One might need something close to Freudian psychoanalysis to get at them. In this connection, Rand's attitude toward emotions appears to be too narrow. She does say that emotions signal valuations but then she also said — on *The Tonight Show with Johnny Carson* — that she is aware of the source of all of her own emotions. That would be a rather gargantuan task to have undertaken, to discover all of the sources of one's emotional makeup, given that emotions begin to be formed much earlier than scrupulous self-awareness begins. (One reason psychology and psychiatry appear to be secure professions is that none of us knows fully why we feel how we do, since early experiences we were not conceptually aware of shaped many of our feelings.)

Free Will

The problem of free will is also dealt with by Rand in a cursory fashion. She held to the doctrine more because it seems that human reasoning, including its errors—evasion, omission—cannot make sense unless human beings are free to choose, to initiate their conduct. Not so much because she had a good theoretical account of free will. She makes reference to the possibility that persons cause their own actions, specifically the actions of their conceptual consciousness, thinking, but this is not developed by her beyond some minimal points having to do not so much with what free will is but with what it is about metaphysics that makes it possible, namely, the reality of multiple causes in nature.

More generally, is the mind a unique being in nature? Rand claims that it is not an irreducible primary, but is it *sui generis*? Or can it be fully understood in the terms of, say, biochemistry or neurophysiology such that terms that refer to mental properties, attributes, activities as such are actually superfluous? A good deal more could have been said by Rand about the ancient mind-body problem.

The Choice to Think

A serious omission in Rand's works is an explication of just what she means by "the choice to think or not." Without Nathaniel Branden's explication of the notion, one would have had a difficult time figuring out her meaning. It is not clear that she truly knew what she meant in psychological terms.

The choice to think for Rand, is a crucial concept, the source of moral virtue. For Rand it is from that choice that one gains credit for doing the right thing—one will, upon having made it in a sustained fashion, gain understanding of what one ought to do, acquire the motivation for doing it, and then do it. Without the choice to think, the element of personal initiative is left out of the moral equation. The ought, as we learned most clearly from Kant, presupposes the can, meaning, if one ought to act thus, it must be true that one has the capacity to initiate what it takes to act thus and it is up to one to exercise that capacity. For Rand, if one refuses ever to undertake the task of living, which first and foremost is thinking, one is out of the moral sphere entirely and will, accordingly, perish. A thinking animal that

won't think is effectively dea[ ] [ ] its humanity and it is inappropriate [ ] good or
bad. (It is analogous to how we [ ] doctor
or attorney if the person has n[ ]

Den Uyl and Rasmussen argue that failing to make the choice for living their human lives is already capable of moral evaluation: one who fails didn't do what one ought to have done. I believe Rand thought that this is not possible to sustain because, prior to the choice, to think, one cannot be held responsible for not doing something one ought to do.

What one ought to do is a matter of discovery; it is not innate. So without the facility, namely, thinking, so as to learn what one ought to do, one is not equipped for the task of doing what is right. Once, of course, one has embarked upon thinking—has made the choice to think—one is committed (again, analogous to how once one has taken the Hippocratic oath, one can be judged as carrying out its provisions well or badly).

Still, this entire area is difficult and for the Objectivist project to be complete enough it needs to be addressed more fully than up until now.[16]

The Nature of Human Evil

Here Rand is far more promising than most philosophers. Few if any have given an account of how human beings can be morally blameworthy. Rand's idea depends on the existence of free will, however, so given that this latter idea is not fully developed, the theory of evil also suffers. For Rand, evil amounts to the failure, refusal, or omission to think, to attend to the world with one's unique form of consciousness. She refers to this as evasion, a kind of willful though not necessarily deliberate "blanking out." And that view does correspond in large measure with how the law and morality in general seems to understand evil: not doing what one ought and has the power to do. Her idea is that living itself is volitional, a matter of human choice or initiative and it commits one to dealing with the world in accordance with human nature, namely, thoughtfully. So when one evades, one is perpetrating a kind of malpractice. Just as someone who takes up a profession is at fault when failing to follow through on what the profession demands of him, so human beings who fail to think about the world and their place in it fail to follow through something to which they implicitly commit themselves, namely, human living.

Rand and Values

Rand raises an interesting problem with regard to value, when she contrasts the value of lipstick with that of a rocket ship. In one way she is committed to saying that the lipstick has more value because all value is indexed to valuers. The girl, who buys the lipstick, being the standard, the lipstick would be more valuable. On the other hand she seems to want to say that the rocket ship is more valuable. But she won't say it's intrinsically more valuable. What do you say? Which is more valuable? How can we tell?

It seems that our first acquaintance with value is relative to us. It is relation to our selves that we can have the minute kind of knowledge necessary to make good judgments. But there seems to be another set of standards that transcends individuals and can serve as a way of evaluating individuals. But I, too, am wary of saying that something like a rocket ship is intrinsically more valuable than lipstick because this seems to imply that its value is absolute. I don't know what is absolutely good or evil. It seems as if the rocket ship is more valuable in relation to what I understand about man and the world and his place in it. It seems as if we can make judgments like this with some confidence while at the same time realizing that we don't know what is good absolutely.

Egoism and Selfishness

Rand claimed that selfishness is a virtue and she rejected protestations that this is misguided since the term means, in the English language, a vice, instead. Rand seems to have thought that what is wrong with the ordinary meaning of "selfish" is that it rests on a history of conceptual confusion as well as the infusion into common moral thinking of the ideas of Immanuel Kant. Critics, however, say, as we have already noted, that whatever the history of the term, it does now mean a vice, a callous disregard of others' well being, not a virtue.

David Kelley has made an attempt to rectify Rand's failure to develop her ethics sufficiently to address some of these issues. In *Unrugged Individualism* Kelley argues that Rand's rational egoism or individualism makes ample room for benevolence and generosity. These are, Kelley holds, virtues because in the last analysis if one is sensibly benevolent, kind, or generous, one will contribute to one's own happiness.

Kelley construes it as necessary to show that a virtue must produce happiness in a kind of instrumental fashion: so that if benevolence did not produce such happiness, it would at best be morally indifferent, at worst vicious. Others have argued that all that Rand needs to make room for benevolence is a dose of Aristotelian ethical analysis—she needs to accept that virtues are not merely means to the end of happiness but constitute something good for the agent, make the agent excellent in his or her humanity. So virtues are both means to ends and ends. Not ends in themselves, of course, for which only happiness qualifies. Generosity is a trait of character that makes of a person a good human being and thus contributes to his or her happiness.

Rand's target has always been altruism, the idea that others are more important than oneself. She simply hasn't addressed the benevolent virtues, probably because she meant to focus on those that clearly enhanced the well-being of or otherwise benefited oneself. She regarded it her task to point out how ethically misguided it is to think of others as of superior importance to oneself. (She clearly has a point: if one is not important, why are others? But if they are, why would one not be? And since one is more favorably positioned to advance oneself than others, that surely could be one's prior ethical concern.)

Still, more work than even Kelley's is needed to clarify the relationship between rational egoism and benevolence toward others.[17]

Evolution and Morality

Rand, a naturalist who found nothing promising about religion, certainly embraced the theory of evolution, at least in its broad outline—human beings as a distinctive species, and life itself, evolved from something not human and inanimate, respectively. Yet, evolution seems too deterministic—most evolutionary biologists tend to either deny free will or, like Steven Pinker, give up on treating morality in a way consistent with and drawing on science, and claim that the world is divided, as Kant had suggested, into two irreconcilable domains.

Rand hasn't directly addressed how evolutionary biology could be made compatible with free will and morality. Not that she might not have done a good job of doing so but it is missing from her works. She has addressed the issue of whether the Christian—as well as some secular—idea of human nature, intimately related to the doctrine of original sin—that is, that human beings have evil and self-destructive impulses that can be overcome only with divine grace or not at all—is true. In *Atlas Shrugged* John Galt, her protagonist, notes that "If man is evil by birth, he has no will, no power to change it: if he has no will, he can be neither good nor evil; a robot is amoral. To hold, as man's sin, a fact not open to his choice is a mockery of morality...." To the ancient question, "Are human beings good or evil by nature?" Rand's answer is "Neither." As she puts it, "A free will saddled with a tendency is like a game with loaded dice."[18] In other words, human beings become good or evil as a matter of choice and are by birth neither.

Aesthetics

The philosophy of art had been one of Rand's areas of concern and she sketched out a fairly elaborate theory of art. However, it is not meticulously integrated with the rest of her thinking and seems to have some lacune in it, such as why should all works of art be judged by the standards of romanticism? Cannot a work of art be quite excellent, yet disgusting? Sad? Tragic?

Another missing matter: What does Ayn Rand mean by the "selective *recreation* of reality" as her definition of art? She doesn't discuss the nature of the art work qua art work, and this is probably because she doesn't have a complete enough theory of how the mind works: she leaves out issues of image and symbol, also of connotation in language.

Rand's idea of the "sense of life" that guides the work of artists is very potent and some philosophers have gone on to develop it but for many the precise relationship of such a sense of life, with human nature as a being of volitional consciousness, is still a missing link.

This notion hasn't gotten much attention, having been marginalized with her aesthetics. It seems to be central to her whole approach. When she condemns philosophers, most of the time it is because of the sense of life that she sees behind what they are saying. What arguments does she give to support her sense of life? Is this the kind of thing arguments can be given for? If as much follows from it as she seems to think, and she cannot give it rational support, then she, on her own terms, has a problem.

Finally, Rand's aesthetics appears to involve a conception of beauty that is completely anthropomorphized. Yet the beauty of a sunset or a flower or the movements of a horse or cheetah seems not to be susceptible to such a treatment. It would have been helpful for Rand to have discussed this in detail.

An "Obligation" to Respect Rights

Why ought individuals respect the rights of others? For Rand, this must be an "obligation" that has a basis in self-interest. There are no unchosen obligations. But it needs to be spelled out. She said a few suggestive things (which sounded contractarian); same for Branden (who wrote about the psychological need to apply principles consistently). But it was not systematically explicated. What they said makes Randian rights different from other rights, which carry deontological obligations of non-violation.

There is a suggested solution to this problem for Rand by reference to the ultimate moral virtue of rationality. To whit, for Rand it is immoral to act inconsistently and to fail to respect the rights of others to make their own decisions, to govern their own lives.

Omissions of Classic Philosophical Problems

The problem of induction

Rand alludes to the problem of induction, but not in detail, probably because she does not consider it a problem. The reason seems to be that this problem assumes that reasoning about the future can be successful only if the conclusions reached are logically certain. But, as we have seen, this idea means that we need always to reach conclusions via the purely formal procedures of logic. Yet, since logic is a method, the conclusions reached when we use formal logic do not rely on either perceptual or conceptual knowledge but on formal symbolism. Once it is grasped that such logical reasoning is but a framework to guide conceptual thinking, and that concepts are open-ended, not closed the way symbols are, it becomes evident that the reasoning involved cannot be expected to mirror formal logical reasoning but must be guided by it. The conclusions of such conceptual reasoning will, therefore, contain concepts that are not finally closed and one can, if one strictly follows the model of formal logic, always conceive or imagine—as David Hume did—situations in which it does not hold. The question is whether such conceiving or imagining is reasonable—is there any reasonable doubt about them?

Gender (masculinity and femininity)

Rand has argued that the relationship of the sexes involves a dynamics according to which men are assertive while women are submissive, at least as far as romance but probably also in other domains (as when she argues that a woman should not want to be president of a country).

There is something here that seems to be plausible, at least as far as the romantic dimension is concerned, since biologically at least but probably psychologically, men do occupy a role in romance whereby they initiate contact and take the assertive position. While women may often play at such a role, it is, some would argue, just *playing*.

But to extend this to the workplace or politics seems a hasty generalization. In order to ascertain that the generalization applies, more work than Rand's on this topic would need to be done.

Rand spoke in suggestively inegalitarian terms about women, though she evidently held that morally speaking women are neither more nor less capable of good and evil than men. She argued once that women should not be presidents; she held that in sexual relationships between men and women, women submit or surrender to men. Is this related to her ideas about the biology of sexual relationships?

Philosophy of law

Rand has argued—actually, more like railed—against anarchism. Her idea that government is necessary and must have a monopoly on the legal use of force leaves open the issue of what kind of monopoly such an institution would be. If it is the kind that some firms achieve through the voluntary exchange of goods and services, namely, dominance but not an exclusive position in the market, then the monopoly position of government need not preclude what Rand found to be totally unpalatable, namely, competition among governments. And in one sense, of course, governments do compete—for citizenship and the presence within their jurisdiction of corporations. A government of a country may not function as effectively, even if it is properly limited in its powers, as does one in another country. So citizens and their various organizations may find it beneficial to switch their legal alliances.

If, however, Rand means by "monopoly of the legal use of force" a restricted or exclusive monopoly, then the question can arise, once faced by Nozick, whether such an institution violates anyone's rights by forbidding competition. It seems to me that Rand is committed only to the former type of monopoly. She could argue that the services rendered by government are necessarily geographically bound— for example, so that the legal authorities can function effectively, travel within their jurisdiction, make arrests, and reach binding verdicts via the adjudicative process. It is possible that such a monopoly is unavoidable, comparable to how it is unavoidable that an apartment house or a gated housing community would be a monopoly— within its boundaries competition would be impossible, even though once terms of exchange have been satisfactorily met, those who belong within the system can depart (use the exit option, as the economists would say).

Still, it is unfortunate that Rand was so impatient about this topic and treated critics or adversaries with so little respect.

Rand and the Family

A serious problem with Objectivism, at least if one defines this in terms of what is present in Rand's novels and nonfiction writings, is the almost complete lack of a serious treatment of parenthood, raising a family and so on. This may not disturb young people who read Rand's novels, but it may well concern adults who would be put off by the lack of discussion and by the difficulty of seeing some of the characters as possible parents. (Indeed, is there any serious and realistic discussion in Rand of being a good husband or wife?)

Nathaniel Branden has dealt with some of these issues but, because she disassociated herself from him, Rand could not defer to his treatments on such topics and needed to address them herself.

Some Other Loose Ends

There are also issues that Rand does not deal with sufficiently, even if her philosophy proper is not directly involved:

Philosophical Exchange

Rand has largely eschewed the discussion and critique of other thinkers' works. Her effort in *For The New Intellectual* simply does not suffice as a sufficiently in-depth examination of the thought of major thinkers. At most it is a kind of loose, symbolic caricature of what Plato, Hume, and others have argued at great length and with considerable astuteness. Her treatment of John Rawls, without actually having read him (by her own admission) is unacceptable. Even her critique of behaviorist B. F. Skinner tends too far toward the polemical, as does most of her work. Of course, Rand, who was shunned by her intellectual peers, may be forgiven for not showing respect toward those who paid none of her ideas any serious heed and lumped her, unjustifiably, with such right-wing groups as the John Birch society.

Relationships between her philosophy and other approaches (Aristotle's teleology, Nietzsche's ethics, Marx's theory of alienation) could have been explored in more detail. Some of her students have made up for this—Professors Allen Gotthelf and James Lennox, Professor Lester H. Hunt, and Dr. Nathaniel Branden—have dealt with each of those philosophers, respectively.

Rand was curt and dismissive of most of her critics, a trait that has garnered for her a reputation as autocratic rather than philosophical in dealing with those who didn't see fit to agree with her right off the bat. Yet, it is arguable that someone who was treated so dismissively by her peers owes little respect in return.

The history of philosophy

Rand's interpretation of the history of philosophy (and of history for that matter) is quite idiosyncratic. This is important because she defines herself against the tradition. Aside from claiming originality for things that were not original (which issue George Smith has dealt with) there are some serious issues associated with this. To hear Rand tell it, the vast majority of humankind has labored under one delusion or another, yet she sees things as they are. Perhaps Aristotle alone had a glimpse of what Rand saw. If this is the case, and if philosophy is as important to living well as she claimed, why wasn't her life less troubled than the lives of the deluded? Judging by what we know of her life there is little evidence that she managed to escape the trials and tribulations of ordinary people.

Exceptions to Rational Man

From a bioethicist's viewpoint, there is another omission in Rand's ethics. She never addressed people with compromised capacity to reason, from newborns to Alzheimer's victims. Examples include the mentally ill. Are their rights different from everyone else's? What of children, who by all counts are a special case, because they have never had the capacity to reason, and their creation may impose special obligations on parents and (some would say, though I would not) on society. Included in that category are the severely mentally retarded.

This omission may be part of the reason Rand is often perceived as cold, uncaring, atomistic. She is none of those—it's easy to find examples of friendship, sociality, and concern for others in her fiction, and not too difficult to discern how they serve self-interest. It is not so obvious, though, how caring for, say, one's own unwanted severely retarded Down syndrome baby rather than abandoning it serves self-interest. Is it a matter of integrity in carrying out an (undesirable) obligation generated by a voluntary act? Or is it OK to abandon the child (easily done with a newborn) since it will never be a self-supporting human being?

Rand considered homosexuality disgusting, though she also thought that Athenian culture of the 5th Century BC was one of the highlights of humanity. Athenian culture didn't look upon homosexual love as disgusting at all.

Rand actually toyed with the idea of animal rights—her personal attorney, Henry Mark Holzer, is a prominent advocate of animal rights and Erika Holzer, his wife and a relatively successful novelist of murder mysteries and foreign intrigue says Rand was not unsympathetic. (In this she resembles Robert Nozick, who as a libertarian also nearly embraced the idea of animal rights.)

Ayn Rand and the HUAC

On an entirely different level, Rand has been criticized for alleged hypocrisy because she took part in the House Un-American Activities Committee hearings that focused on the alleged complicity of some Hollywood actors, writers, and producers in spreading communist ideas in their movies and belonging to communist front organizations. We know this period by the term "black listing."

Rand, who championed both complete individual liberty to express one's views and consistency in how one must act vis-à-vis one's moral standards, is charged with having breached both principles when she took part in the hearings and testified about the way in which Hollywood movies manage to spread communist ideas. As Barbara Branden put it:

> Ayn Rand disapproved of the Committee hearings. But she decided that since they were occurring, and since there was an overwhelming and very dangerous communist influence on movies at the time, and since she understood the form it took, and since the other conservative testifiers would probably not understand how to explain what should be explained—that it was a concerted attack on businessmen and a concerted salute to altruism— she would testify.
> She believed that it was extremely important that the public understand what they were being fed, and this was her chance for a public forum. She was promised that she would be given a chance to present her case in full; the promise was not kept, and she left the hearings when the committee members refused to let her discuss anything remotely resembling a principle.
> She was never very comfortable discussing the hearings. She seemed somewhat uneasy about taking part in them at all, for obvious reasons. She was extremely indignant about the not-told facts of the hearings: that the party cards of the Hollywood Ten—"those poor crucified martyrs"—were presented; and that conservatives who testified and who were not big stars, never worked in Hollywood again—Adolph Menjou, for one. Black list? There sure was a black list. The communists worked under assumed names; the conservatives could not do even that.[19]

It is not easy to tell from afar how someone ought to deal with a moral dilemma; Rand, the ethical individualist, would know this. For her the opportunity to alert people to how awful Soviet life and the communist vision were seemed to outweigh the need to boycott a process that went counter to her principles but was already a fact of life. It may be a bit like paying taxes for those, like Rand, who consider it robbery: Since not doing so will cripple one's ability to speak out against the policy, one should comply but make clear that it is wrong.

Endnotes

1   (Oxford, England: Blackwell, 1989).

2   Op. cit, *The Virtue of Selfishness*, p. 17 (footnote).

3   When the action is aggressive, however, others are justified to resist because it has intruded upon their own sphere of authority, the sphere wherein it is they, not others, who should be making decisions and taking actions.

4   For more on this, see Tibor R. Machan, "The Right to Be Wrong," *International Journal of Applied Philosophy*, Fall 1985.

5   In 1978 Popperian philosopher Larry Briskin reviewed my book *The Pseudo-Science of B.F. Skinner* in *Philosophy of the Social Sciences* and made the objections to it that Barry makes to Rand. He also assumed that if we can only remain ignorant of what is right and wrong, we will have freedom readily secured for us. But this is the same mistake noted above. A very agile reply to this line of thinking is provided in Renford Bambrough's *Moral Skepticism and Moral Knowledge* (Atlantic-Highland, NJ: Humanities Press, 1969).

6   It is no accident that "criticism" is related etymologically to "criterion."

7   William F. O'Neill, *With Charity Toward None: An Analysis of Ayn Rand's Philosophy* (Totowa, N.J.: Littlefield, Adams and Co., 1977), p. 95.

8   For a clear exposition of this point, see Mary Collins Swabey, *Logic and Nature* (New York: New York University Press, 1955), pp. 93ff.

9   R. M. Dancy, *Sense and Contradiction: A Study of Aristotle* (Dordrecht, Holland: Reidel, 1975), p. 142.

10   Martha Craven Nussbaum, "Saving Aristotle's Appearances" in Malcolm Schofield and Martha Craven Nussbaum, eds., *Language and Logos: Studies in Ancient Greek Philosophy Presented to G.E.L. Owen* (Cambridge: Cambridge University Press, 1982). Reprinted in her *The Fragility of Goodness* (Cambridge: Cambridge University Press, 1986). This idea, as well as those of polylogics or alternative logics of the early part of the 20th Century paved the way of the latter part's enchantment with multiculturalist ideas of the kind according to which no culture is superior to any other. It was also the precursor to Richard Rorty's type of pragmatism, whereby independent, objective truth is impossible. See Richard Rorty, *Objectivity, Relativism, and Truth*, especially, "Solidarity versus Objectivity" and "Democracy's Priority over Philosophy."

11   Op cit., *An Introduction to Objectivist Epistemology*, p. 47.

[12] Ibid.

[13] Op. cit.

[14] W. Somerset Maugham, *A Writer's Notebook* (Baltimore: Penguin Books, 1967) p. 145.

[15] One might add to this the idea that Allah, God, or Jesus saves some persons from natural disaster or disease, while others suffer painful deaths from the same. When those who escape thank God, this suggests that those who didn't had it coming, and in millions of cases — especially of infants and children — that idea is morally revolting. Rand and many others who are non-believers invoke some of these ideas in support of their disbelief in God, although, of course, theologians have labored tirelessly to devise explanations for why the way the world actually is can be reconciled with God's existence. For more on this, see George Smith, *The Case Against God* (Buffalo: Prometheus Books, 1973).

There have been and continue to be efforts to link Ayn Rand to some version of theism or mysticism — for example, by E. Merrill Root, "What About Ayn Rand?" in *National Review* (January 30, 1960), pp. 76-77. There are other such efforts I have seen that are in the works but I do not think any of them succeed, not without some highly questionable revisions of various theistic and supernaturalist concepts.

[16] See Tibor R. Machan, *Initiative: Human Agency and Society* (Stanford, CA: Hoover Institution Press, 2000). See an earlier exploration of the issue in Tibor R. Machan, *Classical Individualism* (London: Routlege, 1998), especially chapter 3, "Human Action and the Nature of Moral Evil." Incidentally, among her errors, though this one is just a simple factual one that hasn't any noticeable effect that matters on her viewpoints, is her acceptance of the Lockean theory according to which "sensations" are "integrated into perceptions." Anyone interested in that subject should examine especially, Gibson's *The Senses Considered as Perceptual Systems*.

[17] See more on this in Tibor R. Machan, *Generosity; Virtue in Civil Society* (Washington, DC: Cato Institute, 1998).

[18] Ayn Rand, *For the New Intellectual* (New York: New American Library, 1961), p. 136. (From "Galt's Speech" in *Atlas Shrugged*.)

[19] I received this observation from Ms. Branden *via* electronic mail in December, 1997. In her recently published journals, however, Rand appears to be less uneasy about HUAC than these observations suggest.

Epilogue

A standard criticism of philosophical work that it isn't like scientific work. It does not lead to cumulative progress. No consensus is reached—it does not bake bread, i.e., it is not practical.

Actually, all these are misplaced lamentations. Philosophy is not a special science—there is no presumption in philosophy as there is in the various sciences; all questions are, at least at the outset, "fair game." Even the existence of the world is a problem to be addressed—something on which science has no business wasting time—if only to be rejected in the end.

As to consensus, there is fairly little of that concerning the findings of science—only those close and committed to the task reach agreement, with most others left ignorant of or outright antagonistic toward the findings. (Consider the controversy about evolutionary biology or ecology.)

Then, also, there need be no particular epistemological virtue to consensus. Agreement is a social benefit, not always an intellectual one. Truth may often be the province of iconoclasts and heretics, not of the great majority of humankind, even the majority of those working within some discipline.[1]

Progress, too, is a dubious advantage in philosophy. What if the discipline is unique precisely in needing to revisit nearly all of its central topics each generation, almost in every human being's life? It may well be the condition of the human species—just as Rand argues—that it has no innate knowledge of the philosophical variety. And given, also, the connection between gaining such knowledge and self-esteem, confidence in our ability to make a go of our lives, those basic issues would need to be dealt with by each of us or, at least, by representatives of each generation of us. Thus far all the efforts to bring philosophy to an end have failed. Perhaps this is why.

In any given thinker's career, there can be progress, of course, but that does not guarantee that those who follow will make something of it—they may just have a basic need to go back to the drawing board. Of course, they may pick and choose from past masters so as to render their own work more fruitful. But the fruit may be no more than something from which they themselves and some of their contemporaries will be nourished, however nutritious it may actually have turned out to be.

Ayn Rand wanted to be right in what she thought about philosophical issues, just as have all philosophers, even those who have denied that motivation. Wanting to be right is probably natural to most attentive human beings, seeing that therein lies a potential guide toward a reasonable prospect of success in one's life. Whether one will succeed in this task is not easy to tell. It is worthwhile, however, to look into how some exceptional people have tried to bring off the task. It has been my purpose here to take a look at how Rand did it.

Endnotes

[1]   See, on this score, Thomas S. Kuhn, *The Structure of Scientific Revolutions*, 2nd edition (Chicago: University of Chicago Press, 1970). While Kuhn's inferences from the sociological features of science for epistemology and the philosophy of science are very dubious, the historical record he presents shows just how often consensus is far from an indication of truth.

Index

('n' indicates a note)

underpinnings of, 14
value judgements in, 60
social subjectivism, 7
socialism, 8, 111
Socrates, 64
solidarity-criteria, 7
Solzhenitsyn, Alexander,
11, 83, 110
Sophist, 47
Soviet Union
technological development
in, 107-108
totalitarian evils in, 96
"speculative proposition,"
in Hegel's system, 43
Spencer, Herbert, 106
Sperry, Roger W., 118
Spinoza, Baruch, 135
spirituality, 138
standards, for art, 24-25
Stoicism, ethical system of,
19
Stossell, John, 82
Strauss, Leo, 87-88, 127
subjective egoism, 18
subjectivist stance, on
ethics, 73, 79
substance, concept of, 42
summum bonum, ethical
ideal, 88

T
tautology, axiomatic
concepts, 42-44
teleology, issue of, 122-124
Theatetus, 45

*Tonight Show with Johnny
Carson, The*, Rand
interview, 138

U
underscoring speech, 42, 44
"understanding," in Hegel's
system, 43
Unger, Peter, 98
universalism, of
Objectivism, 20
universals, issue of, 15
Unrugged Individualism,
142
Updike, John, 25
utilitarianism, ethical theory,
7, 19, 105-106

V
value
in Marxism, 104
in Objectivism, 95-96, 141
Virtue of Selfishness, The, 1
virtues, application of, 20
von Mises, Ludwig, 106,
121

W-Z
We the Living, 1, 2, 107
welfare state, nature of, 85-
86
What is Called Thinking?,
44
Wieseltier, Leon, 53n.3
Wittgenstein, Ludwig, 17, 26
Zen awareness, 130-132

Masterworks in the Western Tradition

Editors, Nicholas Capaldi & Stuart Warner

This series is intended to exhibit for the intelligent reader why certain authors, texts, and ideas are the key to understanding ourselves and our relation to the world as well as each other. The series answers the question: what is the core of western civilization? Each volume (approximately 100-150 pages) will be written by one author and will explain the background to the author's work, the major philosophical ideas—especially their moral and political implications, the influence of the author on subsequent thought, the major issues identified and left unresolved, and the on-going importance of the author's ideas. Approximately one third of each volume will focus on a major work of that author. Each volume will have a bibliographic essay. While there are many series on major thinkers, no such series is designed to respond to this theme of the core of Western Civilization and to do so in a uniform format with some consideration of how individual authors relate to other authors.

For additional information about this series or for the submission of manuscripts, please contact:

> Acquisitions Department
> Peter Lang Publishing
> 275 Seventh Avenue, 28th floor
> New York, New York 10001

To order other books in this series, please contact our Customer Service Department at:

> 800-770-LANG (within the U.S.)
> (212) 647-7706 (outside the U.S.)
> (212) 647-7707 FAX
> or browse online by series at:
> www.peterlang.com